CYANIDATION

THE REFINEMENT OF MY LIFE:
A Memoir

Dr. Jennoa R. Graham, PhD; aka Dr. GNP

CLAY BRIDGES
P R E S S

O bless our God, ye people,
and make the voice of his praise to be heard:
Which holdeth our soul in life,
and suffereth not our feet to be moved.
For thou, O God, has proved us:
thou hast tried us, as silver is tried.
Thou broughtest us into the net;
thou laidst affliction upon our loins.
Thou hast caused men to ride over our heads;
we went through fire and through water:
but thou broughtest us out into a wealthy place.

—Ps. 66:8–12

Cyanidation
The Refinement of My Life: A Memoir

Published by Clay Bridges in Houston, TX
www.claybridgespress.com

Scripture quotations are taken from the King James Version (KJV): King James Version, public domain.

ISBN 978-1-953300-75-1 (paperback)
ISBN 978-1-953300-74-4 (ebook)

Special Sales: Most Clay Bridges titles are available in special quantity discounts. Custom imprinting or excerpting can also be done to fit special needs. For standard bulk orders, go to www.claybridgesbulk.com. For specialty press or large orders, contact Clay Bridges at info@claybridgespress.com.

This book is dedicated to God; my pastor,
Thomas A. Pulliam Sr.; my dual-doctorate supporters
LuCretia Goodlow, Joy L. Ellerbe, and ChiKyla Coleman;
and a host of friends and family. Thank you for loving and
supporting me as I run this unfinished race that God has
laid before me. I shall finish with joy (Acts 20:24).

PREFACE

Cyanidation is the process of separating precious metals (gold and silver) from all impurities. They are like the impurities of life that prevent the establishment of building healthy relationships for success. A triptych is a picture with three parts that, when placed together side by side, represent a whole image. This memoir organizes the formative years of my life in three parts to illustrate the foundational events that make me who I am.

Back in the day when I was growing up in the heart of the Midwest, I had no idea what healthy relationships were, let alone how to obtain tools to build successful ones. Now, more than 40 years later and as an educated woman, I am expected to pretend that my upbringing was pristine and that every decision I made and opportunity that presented itself brought forth fruitful results—you know, that Clair Huxtable life.

My mother always said this: "Life interrupts the best-laid plans," and here I am operating without so much as a blueprint. My life was not cultivated in the image and opinions of others, just a praying grandmother and the awkward navigation of survival, fumbling toward a personal perception of success only to learn years later that God is completely and unequivocally in control.

TABLE OF CONTENTS

TRIPTYCH PART 1

Nivea & Popcorn

My earliest childhood memory was warm, comforting, and fluid. Blissful waves of emotion surrounded me as my mind slowly drifted into consciousness upon waking from a sound sleep. The feathers slipping from the blanket that covered me tickled my nose. The smell of freshly popped corn mixed with seasoned salt was in the air. I heard my mother's voice in the other room, softly singing a cheerful melody.

Rumbles of familiar clanks and tinkles confirmed that she was in the kitchen. My stomach began to roar and grumble in response to the fragrant corn filling the air. The sound was so loud that you could probably hear it across the room. *Why haven't I opened my eyes?* I began to move only to realize my efforts were restricted. I was lying faceup in a somewhat awkward position.

I lifted my hands to remove the blanket and its feathers from my nose while trying to shift my body's position. To my surprise, my hand movements were also restricted. My thumbs moved somewhat freely; however, I couldn't spread my four other fingers to grab the blanket. Mittens—my hands were covered with mittens. *Why did I have on mittens?* I chose to use my elbows instead of my hands to shift my position and relieve the now throbbing ache of my lower back.

It was then that I noticed the extreme, unforgiving pressure from the top of my chest to the tips of my toes. I wiggled my toes in protest to confirm the familiar numbness, and I was instantly annoyed. Looking back, I should have been afraid or scared, but somehow I wasn't. This was *normal.*

Now, fully repositioned, I was comfortable enough to resume my efforts to open my eyes, but I couldn't. There was something soft yet firm resting on my left eye, and my right eye was covered with some sort of cloth. I used my mitted right hand to try to push the cloth on my right eye upward toward my forehead.

I could feel the cloth protest my efforts as it snagged on the abundance of ponytail knockers strategically placed around my head. At last I was able to peek underneath the stubborn cloth with my right eye and see the television positioned in front of me. *That's right; we were going to watch a movie as a family.*

I watched in amazement at the screen as a large, beautiful, shiny, black horse (an Arabian stallion) galloped over the crashing waters on a beach. Entranced, I was distracted long enough not to realize that the singing in the kitchen had ceased. I didn't know I was scratching at my rumbling stomach with my mitted left hand until the blanket was lifted and the rush of cool air waved over me all at once. "Oh it must be time for another Nivea rubdown," my mother announced in her singing voice.

In an instant I was vertical and standing in front of my mother, her eyes bright with a big, wide smile spread across her beautiful face. The smile soon faded as she continued to de-layer the child who stood before her. She began with the cloth around my head, gently removing what must have been medical tape before she unraveled the cloth. She carefully navigated the cloth over and under the strategically placed ponytails.

Once the head wrap was undone, she briefly taped the four ends of the medical tape in the shape of an X over the soft yet firm round thing (medical eye patch) covering my left eye. "That has to stay on a few more days." My rising mitted hand was caught mid-flight and pressed securely back down by my side. "No scratching. Prevention is always better than a cure. Be obedient."

My mother smiled at me once again and kissed my right cheek and my freed right eye. Her smile slowly faded once again as she moved on to the next task. She took a firm grip of the silver tab at the base of my neck. The zipper on my cotton onesie slid down with ease. She removed both mittens and allowed me to balance myself and lean on her shoulder while she gently peeled the snug-fitting garment off my quivering body.

The cold in the air was fully upon me, and like a leaf in a turbulent wind, I began to tremble fervently. The trembling was not helpful, and my mother was visibly frustrated as she slid down the next zipper. The zipper on this next layer was attached to a nylon-like skin that fit me like a glove. There were no hands on this skin, and the feet were a few sizes too small. "Be still, my Precious. We can't afford to tear this one." I'd heard the phrase "my Precious" from a book she had read to me, and it made me feel special.

My mother took an eternity to peel this next layer off, inspecting every inch of it as she went. When I was finally free from the nylon skin, she wrapped me in a towel and dunked the skin in a basin of soapy water. I watched as she pressed and rubbed the skin between her hands and rinsed it with a pitcher of clear water. A large floor fan was facing away from us, and she laid the skin across the front of it to dry.

The wrinkly skin blew gently in the manufactured breeze like a flag at half-mast in remembrance of fallen soldiers. I hated the skin and was glad to be free of it. I watched it blow around and didn't notice my mother grab hold of my arm. She had a firm grip on my left arm with her left hand and a heaping pile of Nivea cream in her right hand.

Tears filled her eyes as she whirled me facedown over her lap and began to apply the cream. The burns on my body treated by skin grafts sourced from my legs had completely healed, but physical therapy and daily moisturizing was necessary to keep my skin flexible and prevent it from tearing as I grew older. I felt my mother's tears land on my back and sit there in suspension like dewdrops on a forest leaf during the crowning of the morning sun.

The tears were soon comingling with the cream as she rubbed and massaged my entire body. She then dressed me for bed with the cotton onesie and underwear instead of the nylon skin. I took one more menacing look at the wrinkled skin blowing in the manufactured wind. I didn't see the huge bowl of popcorn covered with fiery red Lawry's Seasoned Salt placed beneath my nose.

I shifted my focus to see my mother's face smiling once again as she handed me the bowl. I held the plastic bowl like it were made of Grandma's fine china as I looked around for my older brother, but he was already fast asleep. Disappointed, I turned to see my mother's face. She seemed to read my mind and answered the question I had not the courage to ask. She leaned close to my nose and whispered, "Yes, you can have the *whole* thing!"

GANGWAY BBQ

The word *gangway* is a midwestern term notoriously used in the Chicago area to describe the spaces between large apartment buildings on a city block. I didn't grow up in Chicago, but somehow the term seemed more appropriate than *breezeway* or *passageway* used in other urban areas. It was dark, very dark, like a midsummer night's dream. Music with a heavy bass line filled the air. The smell of hickory barbecue (Open Pit) danced in unison to the high notes tickling my eardrums while playing tag with the fireflies.

The grass beneath my bare feet was warm and crunchy as I walked, skipped, and twirled. Every one of my senses was filled with this orchestra of life—stimulating, compelling, hypnotic. I heard in the near distance, "Jenny, hide! We're playing hide and seek. Not it!" Still under the hypnosis of the orchestra, I broke into a run and hid.

I crouched down low and covered my knees with my arms, making sure to keep my legs close to me. I couldn't let them find me. *I was good at this . . . good at hiding.* As I settled in my position and waited, the orchestra eventually faded, and the radio in my head switched on. I was two songs in when I realized that no one called "olly olly oxen free!" I perched my head up and tilted it to the left, listening for voices.

I didn't hear anything—no sound, no music, no orchestra, just the smell of the hickory barbecue. Panicked, I stood to my feet and peered around the tree I had been hiding behind. I didn't recognize where I was. The yard looked the same, and the back of the building in front of me seemed the same, but somehow it was not the building that was my home. I turned to my right, and I turned to my left, yet I saw no one, just darkness.

How far had I run? How long was I hypnotized under the power of the orchestra and the radio in my head? I called for my brother. No answer. I called for my mother. No answer. A chill ran up the back of my neck like the icy tingle on the tip of my tongue with the first taste of a Fla-Vor-Ice popsicle. Something was wrong, and I dared not call out again into the darkness.

The fragrance of hickory barbecue was still thick in the air. I looked up to see a hint of billowy smoke pass a dimly lit outdoor wall light high above the entrance of the gangway. The light hung with the authority of a deflated balloon.

My feet were like lead bricks as I took two steps away from the tree. I heard a soft, rustling noise behind me like a breeze blowing through a pile of leaves in the fall. I turned toward the noise and came face-to-face with . . . nothing. There was nothing there. As if on cue, a single firefly appeared out of nowhere.

It was yellow with a green light flickering in and out amid the darkness, providing me a glimmer of comfort that I was not alone. Instantly, the radio in my head switched on again, selecting a tune complementary to the beat of the flickering firefly. I was halfway through the song when the light from the firefly disappeared just as quickly as it had appeared. I took a moment to calm the panic rising in me once again. I felt so alone.

Darkness in front of me . . . darkness to the right . . . darkness to the left. *Where did my firefly go? Why did you abandon me?* I turned around and saw that the deflated balloon light was now behind me. I was in the center of the gangway. I didn't notice that the smell of hickory barbecue was gone. My link back to my home was gone.

My firefly companion was gone, and the radio in my head was now silent. *Do I go back, or do I keep moving forward?* Before I could decide, a dark shadow positioned just out of my line of sight moved toward me with the swiftness of an owl scooping up a field mouse. I was surrounded in darkness once more.

GOOD AT HIDING

I was good at hiding. I had lots of practice, I guess. These days, the music that played during that midsummer nightmare moved from the outside backyard to inside our living room. During those nights, the sultry bass line of the music pulsed like a slow heartbeat, slightly hesitating to deliver life into the atmosphere. "Children should be seen and not heard." I wasn't allowed to go outside anymore, so I sat and watched as the voices drifted in and out of the living room.

There were soft voices with high-pitched laughs, loud voices with barrel-gun guffaws, and low voices with haughty chuckles. I couldn't ask what was so funny. I couldn't ask about the array of glasses and bottles filled with colorful liquid on the table. The smoke that filled the room slowly crept along the walls and ceiling like waves crashing against the shoreline of a beach.

I was reminded of the beautiful black horse I saw on television, galloping on the beach with its jet-black mane and tail tresses blowing in the wind. I wished I had a horse. I imagined myself sitting tall on the shiny back of that beautiful black horse, riding through the waves on the beach. Lost in the image, I began to move to the sultry music now seeping into my body.

I was distracted long enough not to notice that my hands clapped once to the beat. Stricken with panic, I willed my head to separate from my body so I wouldn't move again. Don't clap to the music, don't tap your foot, and don't move. I continued to watch as footsteps came close to the cracked door of my hiding place. One set of footsteps passed, a second set of footsteps passed, and I held my breath.

A third set of footsteps stopped directly in front of the door, and I wet myself. I placed my hands tightly over my mouth and pinched my knees together in an attempt to stop all fluid of movement. I was immediately drowned by light and sound as the door flew open and I was dragged by my arm through the music into another room.

The voice screaming at me was unrecognizable. I pretended my head was not in charge of my body so I wouldn't feel the searing pain. Bad things happen when you are not quiet while the music is playing. I was good at hiding—well, apparently not today.

MONSTER TRANSFORMATION

Our family's move to a duplex on Highland felt real, like a home you would see on television. The front of the house had a brick porch that kept us cool during the hot, midwestern summer. The front door opened to a spacious living room with an adjoining dining room that led to an entryway to the kitchen. In the kitchen was room for a table with six chairs, and the back door led to a beautiful backyard overlooking an alleyway.

The L-shaped staircase led to three bedrooms and one bathroom. From the bathroom window you could see the highway just beyond the alleyway in back of the house. At night, my brother and I watched the cars fly by as if they were the USS *Enterprise* blasting into light speed from the 1960's *Star Trek* television series.

My brother's room was to the right of the stairs next to the bathroom. My room was to the left of the stairs next to our mother's room at the end of the hall. I was a big girl now. I had my own room and my own responsibilities. In my room I could listen to the music in my head as much as I wanted. I could unwind from the pressures of defending the family from adults, negotiating with paramedics, and enduring the teasing chants of "the devil's children" in the schoolyard.

Finally, I didn't have to create a place to hide. I could sit and dream, play, or sleep without worry of strange hands beneath my blankets, prying eyes behind cracked doors, or indecent proposals. I felt like a change was coming; I just didn't know what kind of change.

I was sitting in my brother's room playing with his *Transformers* toy, without his permission, of course. Bumblebee (beetle bug car) was my favorite, but he only had the Insecticon Barrage (insect beetle). I very gently moved the toy parts from robot to insect, each piece clicking and settling into place like a key into a lock.

All was going well, and I was so proud of myself. I got to the last wing, and instead of a click, I heard a snap! It was almost on cue that my brother entered his room and saw the large, green and yellow, half-wingless beetle in my possession. I could see the cloud of fury rise above my brother's head in a nuclear puff of smoke. Hugh Harman, creator of *Looney Tunes* cartoons would be happy with the likeness of my imagination to his work.

My brother, even with his broad-shouldered stature was not a physically aggressive boy. He did, however, give me the worst tongue-lashing a big brother could give his annoyingly destructive yet inquisitive little sister. Shortly after his rant, we both noticed that the shouting downstairs had slowly crept up the stairs and burst into the entire house like a tear gas bomb billowing about every nook and cranny.

Puzzled, we looked at one another and then turned to my brother's open bedroom door. We heard a large slam, and we both jumped; he jumped into the air and I jumped to my feet. Next we heard the recognizable back door to the kitchen slam, and we made a beeline for the bathroom window just in time to hear the back door slam again. I stood in the bathtub on tiptoes and saw a blurred, shadowy figure run through the backyard, down the alley, and left at the streetlight where the backyard met the alley and disappeared.

Another blurred figure appeared, running through the backyard chasing the previous blurred, shadowy figure but stopping at the backyard streetlight. The figure was no longer blurred, and I could see the white garment on its back and the pointed silver object in its hand. The silver object held high in the air resembled a butcher knife, the haunting combination of the moonlight and the streetlight bouncing off the sleek blade.

Again, almost on cue, the figure turned and looked directly at us through the bathroom window. The eyes of the figure were yellow and seemed to reflect the light bouncing off the silver object in its hand. My brother and I took a moment to look at each other in disbelief and nonverbally confirm that we saw the same thing. We turned our attention back to the yard only to see that the figure was gone.

With catlike reflexes, my brother grabbed me by the hand, yanked me over the edge of the bathtub and into his bedroom, and locked the door. We huddled closely as we anticipated what would come next. After an eternity of waiting, we heard anxious grumblings and harsh pounding on the door. Someone was trying to get inside without success. I was terrified and wanted to run away.

The commotion eventually ceased, and my brother and I fell asleep, huddled on the floor. The next morning, I woke up to the breaking down of the bedroom door. An unrecognizable voice entered the room shouting words I was not yet awake enough to comprehend. In a panic, I elbowed my brother in a nonverbal gesture to request help. In the midst of the shouting, a sound was released from my brother's lips that I had never heard before.

The moment the sound presented itself, the shouting stopped. I turned my head to see my mother with tears in her eyes, holding my brother's chin. *What is happening?* I struggled to process the flood of memories of last night and the scene now before me. I slowly sat up to see my brother's left eye swollen shut from a spider bite.

I was in a complete daze as we got ourselves ready to leave the house. We began our day traveling as a family by city bus to the hospital emergency room. My mother was greeted by name as we entered the doors and checked in. We sat in the waiting area eating graham crackers while my mother sang songs to us.

OLD DOG, NEW TRICK

Seasons changed, and my family moved around a lot. I never really knew why at the time, but now that I am an adult, I have my theories. We settled into a quiet basement apartment with two bedrooms. My brother and I shared one room, and my mother occupied the other. It was newly renovated so there was a hint of fresh paint and new carpet in the air. It was a boxy little place with a living room, dining area, and kitchenette.

Standing in the living room, I could see the bathroom door and entryway to the hall of the bedrooms. Life was cheerful and peaceful. My mom was singing again and even making friends. These friends had children my age who seemed to enjoy playing with me. I was quiet and reserved, and it took time for me to open up to other children. I was so used to being mistreated and teased that I never knew if they really wanted to be friends or were just pretending to make fun of me.

One evening, my brother and I had what is known today as a playdate with one of our neighbors. The apartment was different than ours because the bedrooms were side by side and not across from one another. I was in one bedroom with the other children, playing as children do. I walked into the living room area to ask for

16

something to drink, but there were no adults. *Where did my mom go?* I returned to the other kids at play and asked where our parents went.

A familiar, deep-barreled voice behind me stated that they had all gone to another apartment and that he was in charge of us until they returned. He was a man I had seen before a number of times around the neighborhood, laughing and talking with my mom. I smiled and said, "Yes, sir," and he turned on his heel and disappeared into the hall.

I continued to play with the other kids for a while, but then they got too rough and wild. I don't like being around loud and uncontrollable people or environments. The radio in my head turned on, and I decided to follow the melody into the living room and sit on the couch. I was about three songs in when the barreled voice called to me from the hall.

He asked if I would come to where he was and turn the channel on the television. This may seem like a form of child abuse today, but back then it was common practice for adults to use children to turn television channels, pour beverages, or even fluff pillows. Some adults would even call children playing outside back into the house to complete a requested task. Saying no was not an option.

As an obedient child, I entered the bedroom where he was. I crossed in front of the bed where he was sitting to reach the television on the other side of the room. The television was a small, black-and-white box sitting on what looked like a TV tray. I had seen tables like that before in other people's homes when they wanted to eat their food and watch television in the living room instead of the dining room

I took a moment to inspect the functionality of the television. The knobs were silver and small, which made sense why he asked me to turn them. I didn't recognize the faces on the screen, so I was unfamiliar with the show he was watching. My mom and I spent many days watching old shows like *The Big Valley*, *The Rifleman*, and *I Love Lucy*.

I asked what channel he needed me to turn it to, and he didn't answer. There was something oddly familiar and uneasy about the silence in his nonanswer. A familiar Fla-Vor-Ice chill ran up the back of my neck. I took another moment to gauge my surroundings. I had to cross his path in order to reach the door.

I heard the other kids in the next room playing so loudly that I wasn't sure anyone would hear me if I did scream. I placed my hands on both sides of the small television and positioned myself behind it, using it like a shield. To my horror, I saw the body of the familiar, barreled-voiced man, fully naked, standing in the corner of the room not visible through the doorway, staring directly at me. I glanced at the doorway and noticed that the open door I had entered was now closed.

Would I make it if I ran and screamed? Would my brother hear me scream? I stared back at him with the strongest, superman-laser vision glare I could muster. In response he slowly lifted his hands in surrender and promptly stated that he wasn't going to hurt me or even touch me. He promised to let me leave once he showed me a trick he recently learned. *Is he serious?*

I'd seen pictures of Harry Houdini doing stunts in Tarzan underwear. Maybe this barreled-voiced man forgot his costume. Using this logic, I nodded in compliance and planted my feet firmly behind the TV tray with my hands gripped tightly around the sides of the small television for support. For what seemed like an eternity I stared at an act that could now be described as Kegel exercises complete with accordion-like inflation and deflation repetitions for visual effect.

The proud performer then plastered on the biggest smile I had ever seen and asked, "What do you think?" For a split second I was frozen, paralyzed with fear. Then the radio switched on in my head, a fast-paced *Looney Tunes* Bugs Bunny song that carried me out of the room as fast as my skinny legs could move. I nearly broke my wrist jerking at the door handle because it wasn't even locked.

TATTLETALE

A few days later, I gathered enough courage to tell my mother what had happened at the neighbor's place with the familiar, barrel-voiced man. She was standing in the kitchenette, and I was sitting at the dining room table. She was busy making dinner—fish sticks and broccoli, a staple meal for us. She was humming, singing, and smiling as she bustled about this way and that.

The words fell from my lips slowly and methodically like a dripping faucet too rusted to shut completely off. I watched as the smile from my mother's face faded and something else replaced the brightness in her eyes. I didn't recognize this look she was giving me. Her eyes were fixed on mine, and her teeth were clenched.

She pointed toward me, accentuating every few words that came spewing venomously from her mouth. Her final sentence urged me to follow the direction of her extended forefinger toward my bedroom. The music in my head switched on, and the *Looney Tunes* song "Kill the Wabbit" began to play as I slowly followed the path to my pallet on the floor of my bedroom. Sometime later I awoke to loud slams coming from the living room.

Instinctively, I jumped to my feet and called for my mom. She didn't answer. I kept hearing a loud *thud! thud! thud!* I ran through the apartment to the living room and stopped short in my tracks. I watched, horrified, as my mother, under the control of an epileptic seizure, sat on the floor, smashing her forehead against the corner of the dining room wall.

Blood was spurting onto the wall with each blow and pouring down her face and chest, pooling into her lap and dripping onto the carpeted floor. *Mommy, stop! Don't do that. Why are you doing that? Did I do this to her? Is this what happens when you're a tattletale? This is my fault, all my fault. I didn't mean to hurt her.* The music in my head was pounding hard like a thunderous storm. I didn't realize I was screaming until an adult grabbed me and picked me up.

No-Key Latchkey

Now, by the time I was eight years old, I had resolved that I was the family protector, a logical thinker, and the object of grown men's unwanted affection. I would become like my fictional hero Spock, the commanding officer of the starship *Enterprise* in the television show *Star Trek* and played by actor Leonard Nimoy. I will feel nothing and carry no emotion, only logical thought. *Wait! Is it logical to pattern your behavior after a made-up character who is half-human, half-Vulcan?*

Greek mythology, the Virgin Mary, the Antichrist Damien— *why is it that women in stories are always having babies by aliens, mythical creatures, and spiritual beings?* These thoughts that were comingling with the radio in my head were abruptly interrupted by the screeching halt of the school bus at my stop.

The force of the stop hurled me forward, planting my face firmly into the back of the seat in front of me. I gathered my book-bag and my pride and moved forward to walk down the long aisle toward the front of the bus. During my journey, I tripped over a foot and landed on my hands and knees in the aisle. Not looking at the owner of the foot and eager to get home, I said my apologies to the air, gathered my book bag and pride once again, and proceeded to get off the bus.

From the bus stop, it was a short walk across the gravel parking lot and down the street to the fenced-in yard of our Victorian home with a wraparound porch. My brand-new roller skates were waiting for me, and I was eager to get home and skate around my beautiful porch. The vision of my ponytails blowing in the wind was abruptly interrupted by a slap across the back of my head.

I fell to the gravel parking lot. My book bag was ripped from my arm and thrown across the way. I turned my head upward and to the right to see my assailant. I'd never seen her before, but she was so big that her head completely blocked the afternoon sun. She was a soft, doughy figure with no real strength. She must have been trying to show off for some friends nearby. I could take this to protect our family, and I wouldn't feel a thing because emotions are unproductive.

I had to pick my battles and fight only when necessary, and this was not the time. For the next few moments she did what bullies typically do. She thrashed me about like a Raggedy Ann doll. I heard an adult voice in the distance, and all at once the violence ended, allowing me to gather my book bag and pride once more. I took a moment to gauge the damage and only observed scrapes to my knees and elbows.

I slowly made my way home, smiling at the sight of the fenced-in yard and the curves of my beautiful porch. I gently guided my hands up the railing and took notice of the gentle breeze in the air as I made my way across the porch. I released a small sigh of relief as I grabbed the front doorknob. It felt good to be home. Yes, this was our beautiful home. I turned the knob and found resistance. *Why was the door locked?*

I called out to my mother and began the investigative search of peering through each window of the Victorian structure. I heard the sound of a car rolling up on the street beyond the front yard behind me. I turned to see a familiar man in a familiar car beckoning me to get inside. This man lived with us, so it made sense that he would take me to my mother. I went to the car and got into the back seat where children are supposed to sit. Children are to be seen and not heard.

After a few turns, he picked up a man I had never seen before. As this stranger got into the car, he exchanged hand gestures and words with the familiar man that were unknown to me. The car pulled forward, and after a few more turns, we pulled into an empty alley next to a small, dark building that resembled a garage or shed. *There was no way my mother is in there.* I sat straight up in my seat so I could see through the front window.

I caught a glimpse of the familiar man staring at me in the rearview mirror. I heard laughing and deep swallows coming from the front of the car. That same unsettling chill ran up the back of my neck, warning me of danger. Fear began to creep over me, but then the logic started—two against one. This situation is not like the others; I am older and stronger.

The stranger turned to hand me a bottle of brown liquid and asked me if I wanted some. I knew the stinging smell of alcohol. *No fear this time . . . just think . . . get out of this, and run home.* I started begging them to take me home as I slid toward the right side of the car. I tried to gently open the door, but it was locked. I stated that I could sit on the porch like a good girl and wait for my mother to come home.

The familiar man laughed and said they had a better plan for how to wait for her. The stranger got out of the right side of the car, and the familiar man got out on the other side. The stranger placed his hand on the outside handle of my door, and the radio in my head switched on. *This was a time to fight . . . one chance . . . no screams . . . just move.*

The stranger opened the door, and I strategically kicked and swung my fists in a wild, twirling manner while scooting out of the car and dropping hard to the ground below like a ton of bricks. While the man defended his body, I scrambled through his legs and into the open hole on the side of the dark, small building. *Why are you in here? You were supposed to run home!*

While the radio in my head played softly, I heard the voices of my kidnappers near the main entrance of my hiding place. Fortunately, the small structure was filled with stuff from floor to ceiling, and the men were too big to get through to me. After a while, I heard more voices outside exchanging words with my kidnappers, but they were too muffled for me to understand.

Soon my kidnappers begged me to come out, with promises to take me straight home. The additional voices (now closer to the building structure) chimed in and declared my safe return home. The comfort of additional people convinced me to crawl out of the same hole I had used for my escape.

Emerging from my hiding place, I found the stranger in the back seat, the familiar man in the front seat, and the front passenger side door open. I got in, keeping my hand on the door handle and my eyes on both men. I was delivered back home to my mother, untouched, as promised.

SAFETY IN MUSIC

In the late 1980s, my family moved into low-income housing on the far east side of town. At the time, this was one of the most dangerous areas with gang-related murders nearly every week. In the midst of this danger, I saw this move as a new beginning, a chance to start over. How could living in such a notoriously evil area inspire hope? In a word . . . stability. Our time in this home would be the longest we had ever lived anywhere that I could remember.

We lived there among these monsters freely and unnoticed. During the move, my mother was still recovering from the loss of her best friend who had been stalked and murdered by her jealous boyfriend. It was a significant loss that changed my mother in a way I can't begin to understand. It was as if a piece of her had fallen off into an abyss, never to return.

Although she was extremely moody, she was home a lot more and became actively involved in our school's PTA group. I also took a deeper interest in school and reading. I learned that I was good at schoolwork and helping teachers organize class activities. I didn't have to hide anymore and was often rewarded with compliments for high achievement. As the devil's child turned teacher's pet, I was still subjected to teasing and the occasional confrontation by a bully, but all that was manageable.

I began taking a logical approach to the teasing. If they made fun of my clothes, I'd ask the kids if they were going to buy me new ones. If they made fun of my hair, I'd ask them if they were going to get their mom to redo it. I developed a daily routine for navigating to the school bus stop and often stayed after school to do homework or special projects.

School became my sanctuary, and I took every opportunity to get involved as much as possible. We had no money, so my options were limited. One day I was asked to come to the music room during lunch. I was instructed to sit in a chair and take a good look at the instruments that were laid out on a long, wooden table in front of me.

Apparently, earlier in class, the teacher noticed my connection with a classical piece composed by Johann Sebastian Bach and wanted to know where I had heard it and if I was familiar with the song. I replied that I had never heard it before, but it sounded similar to the songs played during the *Looney Tunes* cartoons on Saturday mornings.

I further explained that they were my favorite cartoons, so I watched them every Saturday with my brother. The teacher smiled slightly and walked over to the small record player in the corner of the room. He pulled out an album, retrieved a sleek, shiny, black vinyl record with two fingers, and gently placed it on the player. He took his time positioning the needle just right before slowly lowering it to the spinning record below.

Seconds later I was enveloped by the sounds of violins dancing in the air. I sat back fully in the chair and closed my eyes. The radio in my head was recording every note. Images began to form behind my eyelids—violins gathered in a circle bobbing up and down in a synchronized performance. My body began to sway left to right like a metronome searching for the down beat.

My right hand sprung to life, accenting the notes in a wagging motion. Each finger took its turn to chase the note previously played. My left hand stayed rested on my left leg as if grounding my lower body to the chair as my upper body attempted to take flight. I didn't realize how big I was smiling until the music stopped and my smile abruptly faded. The gentle ache pulling at the corners of my mouth told me some time had passed, but I wasn't sure how much.

The violins in my head dropped to the floor, and my right hand followed. The radio in my head switched on in protest and played the recorded version of the song while the teacher moved back toward the wooden table before me. I realized at once that I was alone in the room and that the door was closed. *How did I miss the closed door? Isn't school supposed to be a safe place?*

The radio in my head turned the volume up as I logically thought through my options. My thought process was shattered in response to the loud clap now resonating throughout the room. The teacher had asked me a question that I did not hear. Now that he had my undivided attention, he asked, "What was your favorite *Looney Tunes* song?" I responded and watched him closely, still seated firmly in my chair.

After a few moments, he stood and took two steps away from the table. He asked me to come to the table and select an instrument to try out. I took a moment to look toward the door again and back at him, and then I rose to my feet. As if reading my thoughts, he took another step away from the table and extended his hand toward the instruments, like Vanna White on *Wheel of Fortune*.

I slowly came forward to inspect the contents of the table. The clarinet was long and slim with silver, circular buttons down the body like a well-dressed man at a wedding. The tip reminded me of a toenail discolored from months of unwashed feet, and the idea of sticking that in my mouth made me nauseous. The flute was a beautiful, silver bullet stretched beyond the imagination, its circular buttons glazed with pearl-like raindrops.

It looked delicate and fragile lying next to the clarinet, like a couple shielding a special moment from prying eyes. The nausea returned, commanding that I dare not separate them. I quickly moved on, scanning the other parts of the table left to right then up and down. I moved around to the left side of the table to get a better look at the ones in the back when a piercing hint of yellow light caught my eye.

I turned toward the source and was confronted with a twisted little figure that was small on one end and larger on the other. The body was small, yet the boldness of its golden coating demanded attention and respect. The figure absorbed all the light in the room and expelled it like a beacon. I reached forward with my right hand, and instinctively my fingers fell into place as if grabbing the hand of my best friend before embarking on an exciting journey.

I was distracted and didn't notice that my music teacher had returned to the record player. I looked up to see him gently placing the needle down on the spinning vinyl record below. He turned to me and said, "With that, young lady, you can play this." A few moments later, I was enveloped with the familiar sounds of Tchaikovsky's introductory song, the theme from *The Nutcracker*.

TRIPTYCH PART 2

Selfish Summer

Life on the far east side of town was now a routine. I knew who to speak to, who to wave to, and who to avoid. The country area was converted into livable space to house the increasing population of low-income families with children. The area was extremely rough with executions, stomp-outs, curb jobs, drug deals, and shoot-outs as common as the streetlights turning on at sunset. Among this treacherous terrain, my mother's illnesses made our family invisible to the general population.

I was never called as a witness to any crimes or so much as questioned by the criminals or cops. As long as I did my homework and chores, obeyed my teachers and mother, protected my family, and kept to myself, all was well. I didn't have any friends, so I spent a lot of time reading, mostly science fiction. I was a motivated member of the Bookmobile club.

I let my imagination run wild as I looked forward to the future. I was starting to spend more time with our extended family. Cousins came to visit frequently and even spent the night. School was out, but I enrolled in the summer session just to keep myself busy and away from the searching eyes of some of the boys and older men on the block.

I loved having a routine and learning new things such as gardening. The Midwest area is big on learning who the future farmers and agricultural leaders are, so participating in the 4-H Club was a huge deal. I spent a lot of time during the summer after my sixth-grade year nurturing squash, watermelons, and green tomatoes. I sat in my designated plotted area of the schoolyard and picked weeds while massaging the deep, dark dirt between my fingers.

The earth was soft and warm from the heat of the sun. I wanted to make sure everything was good before leaving for a weeklong summer camp to Lake Michigan. I had never been away from home before outside of staying with relatives due to emergency hospitalizations or overnight visits with close friends of the family. It took quite a bit of pleading and my brother's intervention to get permission to go.

The trip was sort of a rite of passage into the realm of teenage independence, and I could feel that it would change everything. Little did I know at the time how much. I don't recall the bus trip on the way to the lake or on the way back. My first memory of the trip was climbing a large hill of sand shortly after arriving.

Older teens and young adults swept away our luggage as someone led us through our first team-building activity of the day. With every step, more and more sand found its way into my shoes. As I approached the top of the mountain-like mound of sand, I noticed a mixture of screams—terror and delight. *What in the world am I walking into? Who is terrified, and who is delighted, and why?*

Before I could utter the questions rising in my mind, I was positioned on a small platform embedded in the sand at the top of the mountain-like mound and promptly pushed forward. I felt one hand on my back and another on my head folding me into a tucked position like a skilled gymnastics instructor. I tumbled awkwardly as sand flew in every direction, making sure to enter every hole in my head and every entrance of my clothing.

I emerged at the bottom of the mound, covered with sand from head to toe. I wiped sand from my face and found myself among the screams of terror and delight from my fellow campers. *So this is what teen camp fun is like? Really? This is going to be a long trip.* And it was. I awoke the next day with strep throat, a chilling fever, and body aches. I was down for the count the entire trip. When I exited the bus at the school after the trip, my brother was waiting for me.

This scared me because I had been coming and going from home to school by myself for a couple of years now. There was no need for him to escort me home. Something was wrong. He chatted with me the whole way home, not telling me what was in store. All he said was that mom had been in an accident, but she was going to be okay.

When I opened the door to our home, I looked up to see two dark, red eyes surrounded by pools of blood surrounded by a swollen, black raccoon mask. Below the mask were three inches of white bandage wrapped around a black dot in the middle of what I almost didn't recognize as my mom's face. I couldn't move, paralyzed with fear and anger.

I had been protecting her for years. *Why would someone do this now? Who did this?* As tears ran from the pools of blood to the bandages around what was left of her nose, my mom tried to explain, but her fractured jaw wouldn't let her. A small puppylike wince escaped her swollen lips.

My brother found courage in her pain and told me the story. An old boyfriend had come back while I was gone and accused her of something she didn't do. The assailant had beaten her downstairs while my brother and a few cousins were upstairs playing video games. Fortunately, they all ran the boyfriend off a few punches shy of killing her. The radio in my head began to play, and anger began to rise again, so hot that I thought my ears would burst.

If I had been here, this wouldn't have happened. I could have protected her. Why did I have to be selfish and leave home for a week? I didn't even have fun. If I was sick at home instead of at camp, she would have been caring for me and not given that old boyfriend the time of day—or would she? Doesn't matter. This will never happen again, not on my watch.

THE TUTTLE LIFE

The school year after that summer was pivotal. As I stood at the bus stop for the first day of school, I took a moment of reflection to check my mood. Nature had started its course, and I was blossoming into a young woman. The emotions flying around my home at that time were extremely volatile. Most days I felt like an air traffic controller trying to successfully ground planes to prevent them from crashing. I was tired, always tired, but that's the way the graham cracker crumbled—an everyday norm.

I had to get up early and walk two country blocks to reach the corner bus stop on time. That day, I left all my elementary school bullies behind. The crisp fall air filled my nose as the breeze caressed my face and ears. I was excited and nervous. I couldn't believe I was accepted into the Math/Science Magnet Program at an inner-city junior high school.

Will they catch me? Do they know I forged my mom's signature? The music playing in my head was abruptly interrupted by the screeching brakes of the yellow school bus. The bus driver, a barrel of a man with a healthy beard and shoulder-length hair, was assigning seats to each child as we boarded. I was instructed to go to the back of the bus and sit next to the child he previously seated. I obeyed, carefully placing my backpack between my knees.

I looked over to my left, and the clearest, sterling-blue eyes I had ever seen stared back at me. Her beautiful smiling face was framed in a cascade of brilliant golden locks I had only read about in storybooks. *Is she a princess?* She led most of the conversation as we made introductions and some small talk before the bus driver silenced us for the duration of the trip.

Along the journey, the bus made a sharp left turn, and my face was completely covered in a cascade of golden locks. As I slowly recovered, pulling individual strands from my apparently open mouth, I broke the awkward silence with one simple statement: "It needs salt." We laughed together hysterically, and a friendship was formed. We were inseparable, going to classes, doing homework, playing on the weekends, and even talking on the phone.

She was my best friend, my "sister," and my academic super-hero. Our friendship was legendary and lasted for years until the tides of time, maturity, and life decisions separated us. One of my fondest memories will always be the time I joined her family on their vacation the summer before my life changed forever.

As a middle-class family, the Tuttle crew didn't have much, but what they did have, they shared wholeheartedly. The road trip to the cabin was long, but we had fun along the way, singing songs, listening to music, and stopping to explore the caves. I learned the difference between stalactites and stalagmites and was in awe of the unforgettable colors, sounds, and smells.

I learned many things on that trip, such as (1) I love hiking through the woods, (2) I am allergic to those woods, (3) I am an expert turtle catcher with a worm-baited line and hook, (4) there is a grave out there with my three initials and no date, and (5) the music in my head doesn't have to play every day. Life with the Tuttles gave me a sense of normal I had only seen on TV or read in storybooks.

I had a second home now with two "parents," a "twin sister," and a "little sister." I found out from these parents that it is possible to get married and have a decent—not perfect—life full of love, laughter, and adventure. All men aren't evil, eager to take what they think they deserve by any means necessary. There are safe places in this world, and I had two—school and my second home.

If there are two safe places, then there are more, and living a life without fear of men is possible. I don't have to fear the long looks and leering stares of the boys and men on the block. I have the right to choose. There are men who will love, protect, and provide for their families. *I don't have to be afraid. I won't be afraid ever again.*

LOVE BLOOMS

It was the summer before my freshman year of high school. I opted to attend summer school at the local high school to meet the gym course requirement. I heard that the Math/Science Magnet High School had an Olympic-sized swimming pool and that all the students were looking forward to flaunting their latest fashions and developing bodies in swimwear. I wanted no part of that.

Very few people had heard about my incident as a toddler and even fewer had seen the scars. I had no intention of prancing around a swimming pool in a bathing suit while my classmates stared, pointed, or gasped. In junior high, I had successfully made a few friends and even had small, party-line conversations once a week. My friends saw me as funny, smart, and just enough weird to be interesting.

Thank you, Isaac Asimov, the original story creator of all things science fiction. No way was I going to jeopardize the normality that gave me a sense of belonging and community. So I signed up for summer school and walked the 1.5 miles every day to exercise, swim, and learn health basics with a small group of strangers, the likes of whom I would never see again. *This was perfect.*

Although the area where I lived was considered treacherous terrain, most of the illegal and illicit activity occurred at night. Every morning, I took my time and walked the two country blocks to the main road. I listened to the birds, squirrels, and other animals that dwelled in the landscape. Once at the main road, I looked both ways before crossing the street. The converted country street was lined with modest homes on one side and an empty field on the other.

Years before, the empty field was alive with trees like a small forest, frequently used by many for shelter from danger and evasion from the law. Now that the area was scalped, it appeared cold and unwelcoming, a contradiction to the "Coming Soon" sign prominently posted and announcing the new construction of a church. The music in my head continuously played as I walked half a mile to the next main street.

After crossing the bridge, I took a moment to wave at the Tuttle residence. The modest home sat manicured and erect on its corner lot, caressing the bend in the land touching the creek. "Dad's" victory garden, the firepit, the dog house, and the swing set were clearly visible in the unfenced backyard.

Every so often, I turned down this street and took a longer route to the local high school. That route navigated me through a more residential area and away from the main road where the sidewalk ends, reminding me of the book of poetry by Shel Silverstein. On this particular morning, I chose to go this longer route. I was going to be late, but for some reason, that didn't bother me.

Then a car pulled up slowly beside me. I wasn't surprised since that happened regularly during the warmer months of the season. I paused and turned to my left, ready to give my normal abrasive comment that sends your typical, steroid-filled Macho Man Mack on his way. Instead, what came out of my mouth was . . . nothing.

I was speechless as this man with smiling eyes asked me if I needed a ride. I could tell he was older than me—he was driving, of course—but there was something innocent about how he was positioned in the car and how he spoke. I took a moment to observe his long, lean features; the clean, low-fade haircut; the smooth, baby-face skin; and the prominent Adam's apple at the top of a long neck leading out to broad shoulders.

His windbreaker outfit was zipped and seemed to fit him like a glove. Long arms connected to two giant hands were firmly placed on the steering wheel. Before I knew it, I was in the car being driven to my destination. He seemed absolutely thrilled and relieved that I accepted. He started making conversation, throwing in a few corny jokes here and there.

Was he blushing? Did his eyes brighten while he laughed? Am I laughing with him? I was completely at ease with him. Even though we just met, there was an instant connection. I listened to him talk and returned my gaze to finish my survey of him. His legs were just as long as his arms, and he completely filled the space of the vehicle.

He was a tenderhearted giant, not threatening or demanding, almost shy. He was a nice guy who wanted to protect me, make me laugh, and spend time with me. *You want to see me again? Sure. Why not?*

INDEPENDENT LIVING

What started as a summer romance bloomed into something real and somewhat stable. Our young love was encouraged by some and attacked by others. The opinions of others made no difference to me. I was happy, and that was all that mattered. To my surprise, my biggest cheerleader at the time was my mom. In an area where I could have been dating a drug dealer, gang banger, or even a police officer, my churchgoing man was tall, handsome, loving, and protective.

He was truly a diamond in the treacherous rough, and I was appreciative that he chose me to love. About a year and half later, I discovered I was pregnant with our first child. I wasn't surprised or even scared. I had tried many times to get birth control on my own, but because I was only 15, I needed parental consent.

Unfortunately, my mom who so privately supported our physical relationship somehow didn't approve publicly of birth control. We tried every condom under the sun (so we thought) and always had issues. Now that I am more informed, I know that I have a latex allergy, and he probably needed a premium product that was not in our budget.

Once that second blue line showed up and the clinic lab test popped up positive for confirmation, I was sent home with a brown bag of 50 free condoms and a two-year prescription of birth control pills. The clinic even scheduled a follow-up visit for me to discuss IUDs and other more long-term birth control solutions. *Why wasn't all this available* before *I became pregnant?*

Medically speaking, my pregnancy overall was pretty uneventful until the last few months. I had no plan or clue of what I was doing, but somehow I knew it was all going to work out. I was a logical thinker and could think my way through anything. *Why would raising a child be any different?*

About six months into my pregnancy, my mom got married and moved out of the house. Her husband referred me to a job fair where I landed a job at a billion-served fast-food restaurant 10 miles away from where I lived. I had no car, so two days a week and on weekends I walked the two country blocks to the bus stop and rode the city bus 20 to 30 minutes to get to work.

I was grateful to have work but wondered why in the world someone would hire a girl who was visibly pregnant. I got off the bus and walked a few blocks to the restaurant. Traffic was extremely heavy in this mall area, so I had to be diligent when crossing the street, even at a stoplight. I entered the restaurant and let the cashier know why I was there.

She looked me over, shrugged, and sent me to the back room to wait for the manager. Nervous, I sat patiently as I heard a woman's voice shouting directions at the team. The voice got louder and louder as she approached the area where I was seated. I could hear her, but from where I was seated, I couldn't see her. She shouted out more instructions. She was really close now. Then I heard the sound of papers scattering on the floor.

Instinctively I stood up and moved toward the sound to help pick up the papers. Like a professional football player (Team Peyton Manning for life), I cuddled my modest baby bump and maneuvered through the area only to see that there were no papers on the floor. Puzzled, I looked up to see that the woman had already gathered the papers, which were resting gently on top of my new boss's *very* protruding belly.

She gave me the biggest smile and said she was glad to see I was ready to work. She further explained that she was eight months pregnant and was looking forward to seeing me keep the team on their toes while she was out on maternity leave. *I'm here two seconds, and she already has me earmarked as a team lead. What in the world did my stepfather say in his referral?*

It didn't matter; I needed a job, and now I had one. With this job I could work full-time in the summer, save a little money to prepare for the baby, and go back to high school. I was living alone and paying all the bills except the low-cost rent. I went to work, kept my prenatal appointments, nurtured my romantic relationship, and stayed connected with my friends.

I learned a lot about time management, transportation, and financially managing a home. In my mind, I was independent in every sense of the word. I had my own money, I had my own space, and I took care of my business. Everything was fine for a few months, and then things started to get emotionally complex.

My mother and her new husband moved back home on a semi-part-time basis and insisted I transition to the basement of the home after the baby was born. I was not interested and wanted nothing to do with that plan. *I had everything set in a routine, so why change now? Sure, at this point I hadn't thought about daycare or how I was going to manage finishing my junior and senior years of high school, but one problem at a time, right?*

D-Day (Delivery)

The morning of August 27, 1994, began like any other day. I was scheduled for a prenatal visit, my last one before I would be on 24-hour baby watch. My son was due to introduce himself the next day. I remembered feeling tired and anxious. I was still walking and taking public transportation, but at nine months, I was all beach-ball baby, complete with swollen feet and swollen nose.

I waddled my way to the clinic waiting room and sat uncomfortably in the ergonomic chair. Looking down at my belly, I could tell my son was just as uncomfortable as I was. I placed my right hand on the right side of my belly and gave it a little tap. The child inside responded by wiggling his head. I could feel the hair on his head wave like kelp floating in a large body of water.

I moved my hand a little to the left and flattened it with my fingers spread wide, gently pressing for an instant. The child again responded by placing a flat foot against my hand and gently pressing back. My goodness! His foot was all the way up by his head now. That was a game we enjoyed playing together. I tapped or pressed my belly, and he moved around to touch the same spot.

I moved my hand to the left side of my belly and gave a tap. That was a mistake. The child responded by wiggling his lower half in an attempt to move his foot, but there was no room. I watched in amazement as a visible foot pressed hard against the top of my belly and moved a full inch to the left. The pain was so sharp and quick, I could barely think.

I shifted to my left, placing the child in a seated position and rubbing the right side of my belly where his head was pressed firmly against me. That seemed to make him happy, and he wiggled his head in response. Just then someone called my name to go back to the exam room for the usual poking and prodding. At the end of it all, after nine months of a perfectly normal pregnancy, I received a diagnosis of calcinosis and preeclampsia.

Calcinosis was an unhealthy amount of calcium deposited in the form of a golf ball on top of my swollen foot. Although a nuisance, the calcium would work its way out of my system and disappear. Preeclampsia was basically a case of extremely high blood pressure due to pregnancy-related conditions and stress.

This diagnosis was a little more frightening and gave me a one-way ambulance ride to the hospital. The only way to control or get rid of preeclampsia is to monitor the blood pressure and deliver the baby, if necessary. In a flash, oxygen was strapped around my nose, a magical wheelchair appeared out of thin air, and I was staring at two caduceus symbols engulfed in ambulance siren sounds. As quickly as the commotion began, it ended.

I was sitting in a quiet, semiprivate room with only the beeps of the various monitors to keep me company. I am not sure how long I was there before the familiar voice of my tenderhearted giant filled my ears. *Did someone call him? Did I call him? Does anyone else know I am here?* It didn't matter. It was so good to see him, and I felt comforted to know he was there.

I looked up at him as he proceeded to ask me questions. I didn't like the worry he carried on his face. He was making corny jokes and laughing, but the brightness of his eyes was not present. He stood over me like a protective soldier as the nurse and doctor came in to give us updates. They induced my labor and instructed me to settle in for the night and be prepared for hourly, round-the-clock monitoring. The next morning I awoke in a private room and was informed that I could have visitors.

The birthing contractions had started, but the dilation process was slow. One nurse took a look at the contraction monitor and uttered these words: "Ewe wee! Can you feel that? These contractions are off the chart!" I turned and gave her a look that sent her out of the room. Apparently my incident as a toddler left me with a high pain tolerance and the inability to feel uterine contractions. I wasn't sure if I could give birth or even get pregnant, but there I was, 16 years old, in labor, and full of anger.

Soon more familiar voices came to see me in shifts—those who loved me, those who were worried, and others who were putting on a show to say they came. My emotions fluctuated wildly from happy to frustrated to angry, depending on the visitor. Having reached a predetermined critical limit, the doctor banned certain people from my room and announced that he had ordered a C-section.

It took three tries to get the epidural through my skin because of my scars. After delivery, the medical staff discovered a bacterial infection had grown around my son in the womb. I didn't get to see or feed him for three days while both of us were being treated. For extra fun, my latex allergy was not noted on my chart, so my reaction exacerbated the infection, resulting in the reopening of my C-section incision and an extra 11 days in the hospital for treatment.

The treatment involved packing the incision area with fresh gauze twice a day to allow for healing from the inside out. When my son and I were released from the hospital, we went home alone. In order to continue my own treatment, I removed a sliding mirror from the bathroom and placed it between my knees to change the gauze. During the five weeks it took me to heal, I enrolled in a homeschool program so I could stay on top of my class assignments.

BATTLE FOR EDUCATION

Education is not a right; it is a privilege. I learned firsthand that if you want an education you have to fight for it. I had given birth to my son about five and half weeks ago, and my C-section scar was now almost completely healed. There was only a sliver of tender muscle peeking through the previously reopened incision.

I was sitting at the dining room table finishing up a class assignment delivered by my homeschool coordinator when I remembered that a letter marked urgent from my high school arrived in the mail a couple days before. It was addressed to "the parents of," but since my mom was not living with me and I most likely would have resolved the matter myself, I broke the law and opened the letter.

I read in disbelief as the document before me gave an accurate account of how I had not been in attendance since the day of registration. It went on further to state that if I did not return to school by a particular date, I would be dropped from the Math/Science Program and further action would be taken to expel me from school. I took a long moment to process this information.

How could they threaten to expel me? Right after I was released from the hospital, I arranged to be temporarily homeschooled due to mandatory medical maternity leave. Did they think I enrolled in the day program for adults? A violent shudder ran up the back of my spine. I sat back and thought of the day I was introduced to that adult program. I was about five months pregnant with a full waddle, making my way across campus.

I was led to a specific building dedicated to cultivating domestic living and trade skills for adults seeking nontraditional education as they prepared for the workforce. The concept sounded wonderful for an expectant teen mother unsure of her future. I was informed there were specific classes designed for maintaining a household and properly caring for children.

The offer was sweetened since there was a half-day curriculum. I would be free to take some elective classes with my friends in the afternoons and still graduate on time with them. The music in my head was drowning everything out as I began to think about what this new schedule would possibly look like and what combination of classes was available. As we rounded a corner to enter a room, the music in my head stopped short like the scratch of a DJ's turntable.

Not five feet in front of me, two girls who looked younger than me were screaming and swinging their fists at each other. The momentum of their swings eventually caused them to collide and fall to the floor, entangled. Fights at my high school were not new. My classmates and I even wrote articles that were published in the newspaper about the level of violence we observed.

This particular fight completely stunned me. The two young ladies were both *very* pregnant—about-to-deliver-any-day pregnant—and from the screams, I could tell they were accusing each other of stealing their man. This was four years before the 1998 R&B hit from Brandy & Monica called "The Boy Is Mine." Um . . . yeah . . . no, I will find a way to stay in the magnet program. Thank you very much.

I was distracted in my thoughts long enough not to hear the first few faint cries of my hungry son swaddled on the floor pallet. I slowly slid from the dining room chair to the floor and crawled toward him. At the sound of my voice, his bright eyes popped open, and he began to coo. I gently scooped him up and positioned myself as nursing mothers do and commenced with mealtime. His little hand grasped my forefinger and pulled it close to his suckling cheek.

I smiled and playfully tapped his kung fu grip with my opposing thumb. I thought about my approach to solving my latest problem. My medical leave would be up soon, so my first step should be to contact my homeschool coordinator and discuss the letter.

STAND YOUR GROUND

It was a rough time, but I successfully got back in high school with no time lost, and things seemed to be holding together pretty well. I had everything worked out. Most days, my gentle giant picked up my son and me in the morning and dropped us off at the daycare. I then took the school bus from the daycare to the school. On the days we were late, I had to catch the city bus.

After a full day of flexing my academic muscles, I took the school bus to the daycare, and the daycare driver brought us home. I was blessed to be accepted into the Vivian Smith House Teen Parenting Program. It was designed to help teen mothers meet daycare and transportation needs in order to finish high school. I lived so far away from the program that their budget could only accommodate one-way transportation for me, after school.

I was further blessed to get a job within 45 minutes walking distance from where I lived and another local daycare that provided 24-hour service. Every week I gave my evening daycare provider my work schedule. On the days I had to work (30 hours or more per week), she picked us up from home and gave me a ride to work. After my shift, my gentle giant picked us up and drove us home.

Contrary to popular belief, my gentle giant and I still lived in separate residencies because we were not yet married. I managed to get my homework finished during my work breaks and after my son's bath-'n'-bottle bedtime I averaged about three to five hours of sleep per night with a 5:00 a.m. wake-up call.

All things considered, I had a pretty consistent schedule until the day the earth stood still. The winter months were upon us, and my bright-eyed bundle of joy was growing into a heavy package of joy. He had completely filled out his carry-all from the top of his head to the end of his long legs that protruded forward like two prongs of an engaged forklift.

My mom, who had decided to move back home on a semi-part-time basis, began making more executive decisions regarding her now stereotypical "hood rat" of a daughter. In previous conversations, I had stood firm in my decision not to move into the basement of her and her husband's home. I had everything worked out and had not asked for any assistance from them, so logically there should have been no consequences as long as I was taking care of business.

Unfortunately, my mother was trying to ensure the financial stability of her grandchild and prevent the production of any more babies while I was under her semi-part-time roof. It had happened—I was so distracted by focusing on finishing school and caring for my son that I had unknowingly entered the child support zone.

The radio in my head started playing the theme song to Rod Serling's 1960's hit television series, *The Twilight Zone*. The introductory phrase, "You're traveling through another dimension," echoed through the haunting melody on a torturous loop. And with one parental maneuver, I temporarily lost my stability, my romantic relationship, and my composure. What was my next course of action? Ignore her and soldier through the pain.

I adjusted my schedule and started taking public transportation again. Like a skillful, flying trapeze artist, I perfected the delicate balance of school books on my back, a diaper bag on one arm, and my heavy package in his carry-all on the other arm. I did all I could in every way that I could to logically think through my problem.

I made it to work, stayed on top of my grades (except for calculus, my academic superhero to the rescue), maintained my home, and took good care of my son. He was happy, healthy, and strong. I was tired, angry, and barely making it through each day. I had two choices: find a way to survive and go away to college, or give my son up for adoption.

INTO THE WOODS

My senior year of high school was a complete blur. I did what was expected, accomplished every task, and took great care of my son. I received many compliments on how healthy and happy he was. He was always smiling and laughing. I was glad to hear it, although I didn't really notice it myself. I was like a robot on autopilot, and as long as nothing major happened, my programming was fully functional.

After a while, others who knew of me or interacted with me began engaging me and interjecting themselves into my life. Outside of the people who already loved me, the doctors and nurses at my clinic became more involved and conversational during my two years with them. My son's pediatrician challenged me to familiarize myself with medical terms and avoided the use of common language.

My male nurse always took great care of us during our clinic visits and even arranged a graduation party for me. I knew I was graduating from high school, a bump in the rearview mirror of my life. What I didn't know was if, where, or how I was getting into college. I was so focused and stressed about my future that I was completely alienating my classmates and friends.

I remember sitting in science class listening to the infomercial-worthy razzle dazzle about the latest in spectrophotometer instrumentation. Our brilliant science teacher, who looked like the first cousin of Mr. Miyagi from the 1984 movie *The Karate Kid* starring Pat Morita, was completely enthralled with terms like monochromator, wavelengths, and cuvette. I admired his passion and love for the art of science; I shared it at that time.

I was watching intensely as his hands hovered precisely over the instrument, accenting important sections with a point of a finger or a flick of his wrist. I was distracted long enough not to notice the firm grip that closed on my wrist. In an instant I was lifted from my seat and half-dragged, half-run into the guidance counselor's office.

An application and a pen were planted loudly in front of me, and instructions were directed at me to complete it. It was said with more authority than I had heard outside of marching band practice. I took a moment to read the header before getting started—Dale Davis Scholarship.

Time rolled on, and the buzz began to pick up about prom and other senior-related activities. I stepped off the school bus and entered the Vivian Smith House. A young lady working there greeted me with the wide smile of victory. She had heard I wanted to go to college and knew I needed access to family housing and a daycare for my son.

She knew the perfect place, a large private women's college tucked away in the corner of a small town 83 miles west of the metro area. That distance might as well have been the end of the earth. I had no means of transportation, and I didn't have the money to take the SAT or ACT. She told me not to worry or make any decisions until she took me there to check it out.

I don't recall the drive or the conversation on the way there. My first memory of the area was the smell of the trees and freshly cut grass. The front gates were standing tall like a fortress wall, cradling the entrance to the avenue like a warm embrace.

My hostess and I walked the entire campus, and I took in all there was to behold. I could faintly smell the distinct scent of horses in the distance and hear happy children playing nearby. The buildings stood erect and manicured, almost preserved from the passage of time.

The most prominent of all the buildings was the campus church consecrated in the early 1900s and kept in full representation of its immaculate name. I felt like I had walked onto a reenactment of history and that my participation would add to a legacy that had not yet been forged.

This feeling was further solidified with the campus mantra lyrics, "Whose woods these are, I think I know," inspired by the 1923 Robert Frost poem, that rang out into the air and pulled ever so gently on my heart. It was everything I needed and more.

God worked in my favor to get accepted to the college and become the first recipient of the Dale Davis Scholarship, which covered a portion of the cost. I had won a few battles, but the war of life was fully engaged, and it would be a full year after graduation before I made my escape into the woods.

TRIPTYCH PART 3

Social Caterpillar

Social butterfly—um, no. More like social caterpillar. I have never been one to demand or command attention and often prefer the company of a good friend when embarking on an evening adventure. Solo missions into the night are rare and undeniably resemble the life cycle of a caterpillar. The egg phase represents my private thoughts and feelings about wanting to socialize. This phase lasts about two to three weeks or, in the case of winter, two to three months before breaking out of my head and actually making plans.

Like the ravenous caterpillar feeding its growing body, I spend a lot of time consuming information to determine my next social debut. I also consider any necessary changes in my wardrobe to accentuate certain features. External substances such as lotions, potions, and fragrances are also considered to enhance or complement my body's natural chemistry. The research in this caterpillar phase is delicate and must be thorough, down to the last miniscule detail.

The duration of this extensive research depends on the unique mix of event quality and affordability. Once a suitable venue is chosen for the social debut experience, the presentation preparation begins. Hair, outfit, makeup, and shoes are all coordinated with care to fit the occasion.

I confidently enter an establishment and take my first stroll across the room with all eyes on me. And then it happens. The small-group conversation begins as all conversations do, with introductions, a few smiles, and a dash of nodding and laughter to signify active listening. Depending on the audience, my first name causes a pause since its pronunciation can be considered difficult. Those who have traveled internationally and are familiar with cities in Italy or even cured processed meats have less trouble. A semi-personal yet socially acceptable question leaps into the air with the grace of a skilled ballet dancer.

What was your childhood like? The challenge is accepted as a voice to my left begins to embark on a fascinating narrative. As the radio in my head turns on, my version of the fact checker character from the 1991 sitcom *Herman's Head* races through the compartments of my mind to find the unique combination of appropriate yet socially acceptable responses.

The little character in my head dashes back and forth between checking compartments and turning off the automated radio that keeps turning on without my permission. I can't hear anything with that radio going. A dull ache begins to form at my temples as I struggle to balance listening to the narrator while approving or rejecting the information the little character in my mind retrieves.

Now the small audience has turned to me for my contribution to the conversation. The little character slowly comes forward to present the memories gathered from the corners of my mind. (*Barbra Streisand? Focus, woman!*) I take a deep breath, part my lips, and begin my narrative. I can tell from the facial reactions that the information is not well received. There is confusion, horror, and even disbelief.

I thought this time would be different, so I excuse myself from the group and find a quiet spot to transform into a caterpillar pupa. From the safety of my social chrysalis I observe others and recuperate. In most cases, this is the end of my social life cycle for the evening. On occasion, when alcohol is involved or I am in the comfort of close friends and family, I relax enough to fully develop into a social butterfly—witty, elegant, and even alluring.

This common practice of retreating to a social chrysalis all changed when I met and befriended an enchanting woman dubbed Ms. Jewcee and was welcomed into the bosom of her posse. In a particular and unlawfully specific social environment, I learned a lot about myself and how to be an impeccable hostess, catering to the needs of others.

I was so loved by this band of illegal misfits that I was given a "family" nickname that I so proudly and permanently etched into my skin. For a span of time in certain non-business circles, I was known only as Blaque Cherrie, the social butterfly.

LESS THAN ASTUTE

Admittedly, in my teens and 20s, I did not always make the best decisions. As an adult, I understood that the less astute choices in life that are made during those years are engineered and piloted by an underdeveloped brain fueled by hormone-soaked emotions. So what happens when an underdeveloped brain steeping in an abundance of hormones is emotionally suppressed? It is a dangerous mixture of life-threatening nonsense and foolery wrapped in a mask of social exploration sprinkled with experimentation. Outside of my childhood experiences, there has only been a handful of times in my life when, after leaving my place of residence, I was not certain I would live to see the next morning (e.g., boarding the entourage tour bus at a DMX concert or getting roofied at a mansion party).

During my continuous role rotation of student, mother, care-giver, and family provider, the pressures of life burst like an over-inflated balloon. The aftermath left a noticeable mess. I remember clearly how the stadium seating was extremely uncomfortable as I attempted to pull down the borrowed skirt that was too short to protect my thighs from the pinch of plastic trim.

The crowd was slim, and the female musical artist performing on stage was uninterested in her audience and paced like a distressed lioness. After working 70 hours and completing the external degree assignments for the week, I was encouraged to take a break and celebrate my birthday. Getting an early start on my college studies was a much-needed distraction to keep me focused on my future.

During the summer months, the city was alive with events, expos, and festivals. I sat quietly, half-engaged in conversation and half-watching the people around me. I was new to this environment and followed my leader, taking in all the sights and sounds there were to behold. At the end of our evening, I was guided into the back seat of a chariot as my leader gave instructions to the driver and his companion for our next destination: home.

Conversation and laughter began to flow as we shared stories of previous encounters earlier in the day. I was distracted long enough not to notice that we were headed in the wrong direction. At a time when we should have been nearing familiar territory, the chariot entered a dark area known for unsavory conduct.

Upon further inspection with my view limited by tinted windows, I realized we had arrived at a hotel. The music in my head began to play softly as I turned to my leader for guidance. It was then that my fearless leader confessed that this arrangement was impromptu and that we were now at the mercy of two complete strangers.

The music in my head stopped short, and a red light flashed before my eyes, accompanied by a loud ringing in my ears. *Is this the feeling of blind rage? Focus . . . use logic . . . now what . . . how do we get home?* Relying on my previous kidnapping experience, I encouraged my fellow captive (demoted from leader) not to leave the vehicle and to just stay put.

Maybe our kidnappers were just out for a good time, and if we spoiled their fun, they would eventually ditch us. To my dismay, we were driven to a few other destinations before arriving at yet another unsavory location, a nightclub known for large-scale violence and death. The parking lot was well lit, and just as I thought, our kidnappers abandoned us and went inside to partake in the nightclub activities.

Two older gentlemen in the vehicle next to us were preparing to leave the area for the evening. They happened to overhear our situation and offered to take us home. Reluctantly yet cautiously, I accepted and convinced my fellow captive that it was better to take a different risk with older men than continue on the current path that was not working.

The men's wedding bands indicated there was someone expecting them by a certain time, which in my mind increased our chances of a safe and timely transport home. I climbed into the back seat and secured my seat belt. I heard the other doors of the car shut and grabbed the passenger's hand next to me for support.

To my surprise, it was not the hand of my fellow captive-now-fugitive but the hand of a married gentleman. To my horror, I saw my fellow fugitive in the front passenger seat and instantly felt the length of the car double, pushing me farther away from my companion. Despite the wedding ring, the small gesture was perceived as an invitation by the inebriated recipient.

I didn't want to embarrass him for the misunderstanding or jeopardize our ticket home, so I played along. I was tired, afraid, and ready to get home to my son. In this #metoo moment, I was grateful that out of respect for our age difference, he limited his efforts to an eighth-grade, second-base level of exploration.

MATRICULATION

I imagine my college years were really no different than anyone else's. We all did our best to make friends, build networks, have some fun, and graduate on time. The process of education and developing good study habits was never a problem for me. As a goal-oriented person, I excelled at completing homework, tasks, and projects. Presentations, exams, and quizzes were (and still are) my kryptonite.

My biggest challenges came from interacting with others and trying to develop relationships while raising a child during the most immature era of my life. Getting involved in the life of others and letting them into yours can be a frightening yet rewarding experience. Although I won't speak on every event during those formative college years, there were a few noteworthy occasions that resulted in positive, long-term effects.

I had just received a phone call on my dorm room landline asking me to pick up my son from daycare. It was the third call that week, and I hadn't had time to study for an upcoming exam. As I briskly strolled across campus, the five-minute walk gave me time to cool down. This behavior had to stop, but spanking him didn't seem to be working.

I entered the daycare doors and collected my little screaming red face with bright eyes overflowing with a river of tears. As I picked him up, he wrapped both arms and legs around me. *Wait! He's* never *done that before.* With his backpack in one hand and a soft song playing in my head now humming on my lips, I walked aimlessly out the doors and onto the campus grounds.

I was not sure how long I had been walking, but the resonating sound of church bells snapped me out of my trance. I hadn't noticed that I was standing inside the doors of the Catholic sanctuary. I made my way to the nearest pew like so many theatrical cinematic scenes in popular movies. My sobbing child was still clinging to my body like his life depended on it.

After a time, I heard a voice say, "Talk to him." I was not sure if I was hallucinating or if someone else in the sanctuary was speaking. I took a moment to look around before making my way to the women's restroom, my son trailing on tiptoe at the end of my hand. It was then in that unconventional environment that I received a full revelation of the intelligence and emotional strength my son possessed.

He had previously been diagnosed with a communication disorder that identified a disconnect between his speed of thought and his verbal expression. I assumed he wasn't capable of expressing himself. He didn't talk much and relied heavily on hand gestures and facial expressions. However, on this day, I followed the voice of instruction that I now know was God, and I talked to my son as an adult. I explained our situation, what I was trying to accomplish, and how his behavior was counterproductive to achieving our set goals.

I stated that as his mother I must understand the problem in order to make a change. I asked him, "What is your problem?" I stood there for two full minutes while the contents of our one-way conversation processed through his three-year-old mind. In five words, shouting from the top of his lungs with all the authority his 25-pound frame could muster, he changed both of our lives and our relationship forever. "You took my daddy away!"

∞

My second year on campus was a little easier. My son and I had a good routine, and we had a plan. We were happy, my grades were good, and I was looking forward to getting married and growing our family post-graduation. Valentine's Day had passed, and my son's father and I were reconciling our differences and placing all our issues in the past so we could start over.

My Spanish teacher was excited about my progress and asked me to consider declaring Spanish as a minor before graduation. If I did well on the exam early the following month, she would write a recommendation for the declaration and some other academic benefits. On the morning of the exam, the alarm went off, and I could hardly move.

My head was pounding, my arms felt like lead weights, and my body ached from my waist down. I thought I had the flu, but I was determined to make it through the day. I instructed my son to get ready for school while I tried to get myself together. I rolled over and instantly recognized the familiar feeling of starting my menstrual cycle, but something felt off and extremely uncomfortable.

I waited until my son headed down the hall for breakfast and then made my way to the adjoining bathroom. My feet were bricks of cement, making me shuffle like an elderly woman. I ran a hot bath and carefully disrobed from my night wear, letting the one-piece garment fall to the floor. I cleaned myself thoroughly and let the water out of the tub.

It wasn't until I turned to get my towel that I noticed the trail of large blood drops on the ceramic floor leading back to the hardwood floor in my bedroom. Heavy periods and fibroid tumors ran in my family, so I chalked it up to getting older and that life was happening. I made a mental note to call my mom later.

I slowly got dressed, tossed my nightgown in the sink, and cleaned up the floor just in time to walk my son downstairs to the bus stop out front. I returned upstairs and washed my nightgown in the sink, hanging it on the towel rack to dry. I had an hour and a half to study for my Spanish exam.

I went to the bedroom to make my bed. To my dismay, I came face-to-face with what appeared to be a crime scene. I don't recall ever seeing that much menstrual blood before, but oh well, if this was the new normal, I would make any necessary adjustments. First things first; clean up this mess.

I threw out the bed sheet, scrubbed the mattress as much as I could, and went to study while it dried. Thankfully, my Spanish class was in the same building as my dorm suite, so I didn't have far to go. I would just take the exam and lie down on my couch to rest a bit before calling my mom.

I made my way to the classroom and got seated with the headphones to start the exam. After a few moments, I felt a light tap on my shoulder. My Spanish teacher was looking at me very strangely and mouthing the words, "Are you okay?" I slid off the headphones and assured her that I was fine and would rest for the day after taking the exam.

She reached beyond me, turned the machine off, and said, "You're green. Go to the nurse . . . now!" I started to protest, but the look on her face indicated that resistance was futile, so I complied. I sat in the nurse's office and answered all her routine questions as amicably as possible.

She took a long pause and asked me about the last time I had had sexual intercourse. I was honest and told her around a month ago when we celebrated Valentine's Day. She took a second pause that was very long, and I had to ask her if she was okay. She didn't say anything at first and just stared off, lost in her thoughts.

She looked at me with pain in her eyes and asked, "Do twins run in your family?" Puzzled at this line of questioning, I instinctively nodded since twins ran on both sides of my family. I opened my mouth to speak, but before the lost words could emerge, the nurse leaned toward me, grabbed my hand, and said, "My dear, it is my medical opinion that you have just experienced a miscarriage."

∞

By the time my senior year of college rolled around, I had pretty much made a place and a name for myself. I had friends, foes, and others of the spectrum in between. To protect my son's academic future, I made the difficult choice to leave him with my mom while I finished college. I was graduating a full semester early, and he needed the best start for kindergarten without changing schools in the middle of the year.

I was focused on graduating, passing the CPA exam, and starting a new life. Without my son on campus, I began to observe people more and understand how they operated. I also noticed how the school administration handled business, public relations, and student affairs.

During that year, changes in financial aid availability and CPA exam requirements increased both my cost of education and my stress. I was too overwhelmed to handle the situation, so I decided to postpone my CPA ambitions and just enjoy myself for the remainder of the semester. Without the added responsibility of my son, I focused more on social exploration and spent time learning the Greek life.

I noticed that the more I tried to socialize, the more I behaved like an overprotective mother. I monitored, looked out for, questioned, and even reprimanded those in my company during our outings. There was one particular outing that changed the way I viewed myself and gave me a sense of the level of authority I carried when I was provoked.

At this particular outing, I was standing, dancing, and conversing while sipping on the house beverage—alcohol, of course. I was typically the driver, so I limited myself to one cup. I scanned the environment to see my companions enjoying themselves in different locations. I moved around the house making light conversation and encouraging other attendees to try the latest dance moves. On my second round, I noticed that I didn't see some of my other companions.

Unashamed, I started asking around, despite the avid protest of my target audience. One attendee gave in and pointed me in the direction of my missing companions. I stood at the locked door and called out to them. They answered, confirming their safety. Thank goodness! At least some of them were together. I took a few steps back and sipped on my cup, now half-empty.

As I swayed to the slow molasses pulse of the music, as my mind drifted to other times and other places, my thoughts were abruptly interrupted by a door hitting me from behind—*hard*! I turned to see more young men than I would have liked rush through the open door and down a short flight of stairs to the basement. Only one thing could make a herd of young and most likely inebriated men corral like that.

I called out to another companion just to get a reaction. To my horror, she answered with an accompanying male champion orchestrating the initiative. Instantly, I went into what is now known as Mama Graham mode. I demanded my companion be released and brought to me, and I wasn't standing for anything else. I stood my ground and threatened to come down there to start a brawl.

After a few moments, my companion appeared, followed by a sea of disrespectful rants and a shower of thrown beverages and food. As we made our way to the door and onto the freshly cut lawn, the morning sun greeted us and our other missing companions, and we started our journey back home.

∞

Graduation was a very weird time. I was trying out a new relationship, my friends circle was changing, and I had to decide whether or not to accept a job offer in Colorado. Friends and family had traveled far to come and see me, but I was so into my own issues that I couldn't enjoy them or the moment. That was wrong, and I truly regretted my attitude, behavior, and any hurt I may have caused.

I just wanted the day to be over and the next chapter of my life to begin. I ended up not taking the job in Colorado because my son was so excited to be reunited with his father, even if we weren't together anymore. The vision I had for my life was shattered into an unrecoverable thousand pieces, and I had to find a way to move forward.

FRESH OUT

My first year out of college was a definite learning experience. I shared a three-bedroom apartment with my brother and a mutual friend. This was my first time as an adult living under the same roof with roommates. The job market in 2000 was very rocky with the fear of a Y2K technological blackout running rampant throughout the land. Upon graduation, I returned to my seasonal job at a well-known grocery store and also worked part-time at a prominent tax preparation place.

Even with two jobs, I was barely able to maintain, and I didn't get to see my son very much. I am not the type to use people or ask for anything, so I sought no financial assistance other than the child support I received. Exhausted, I was standing in the customer service booth at the front of the grocery store, waiting on the next customer.

A nicely dressed, middle-aged woman who I had often seen in the store over the years approached the counter and slid me two pages of a document. I reviewed them and confirmed that she needed fax services. With a smile, I picked up the pages, completed the service, and returned to the cash register to ring up her $2.00 transaction fee.

I restated the amount and placed my open hand toward her to receive payment. Instead of placing the $2.00 in my hand, she tossed a $100 bill on the counter. Emotionally irritated yet maintaining my smile, I slowly pointed to the sign to her left that stated bills larger than $20 will not be accepted. This was an active store policy that had been in place for decades.

I know this woman knows this rule. What is her malfunction? I picked up the $100 bill and placed it on my open hand toward her while asking for a smaller denomination. The customer refused the bill, crossed her arms, and took a step back. My smile faded slightly as I explained that I could not accept the bill and offered to pay for her transaction myself.

I placed the $100 bill on the counter, slid it toward her, and proceeded to reach into my back pocket for the exact cash needed for the transaction. The customer aggressively approached the edge of the counter and yelled that she didn't need my money and that I would accept her money and give her the correct change. My smile faded completely, and I walked to the right and sat on the bench inside the inner office where cash was counted.

The manager on duty looked at me, puzzled, and asked what I was doing. In response, I folded my hands and placed them firmly on my lap. I raised my gaze to look my manager square in his eyes and said, "That customer is crazy, and I will not go back out to the counter until she is gone." That was the day I adopted this philosophy: I don't want to, and you can't make me.

The next week, I applied for and was accepted into an MBA program for working adults at the local technical college. My logic was that if I was going to miss spending time with my son, I had to make every minute count for something better and not deal with foolishness. Soon, things took a positive turn, and I landed a career-oriented job as a full-time accountant and even built my first home the following year.

WORKFORCE

Life in corporate America was rocky for me. I never really seemed to fit in, and I always had the drive to do more than just my assigned duties. I am a problem solver and love to help. As I already mentioned, I entered the job force during a time of uncertainty and technological unrest. Just beginning my MBA educational journey, I was highly motivated to seek opportunities that would lead to management.

With the assistance of an employment recruiter, I was presented to an insurance company that was looking for entry-level employees who could enroll in an internal management training program after two years with the company. I was overjoyed and couldn't believe my luck. According to the timeline, I would be done with my MBA program a few months before enrolling in the company's training program and placed in a management position upon my successful completion.

I am a very hard worker and skilled at completing tasks and projects with excellence, so I was confident that I would be an impressive candidate. The terms of employment were set and agreed upon, and I was happy—truly happy. Then, since life happens, my world was shaken, not necessarily just stirred.

During my first two years there, the 9/11 terrorist attacks happened, the company filed for bankruptcy, and a new CEO was introduced, which changed almost the entire C-suite level of leadership. Those changes naturally or typically came with organizational changes, and one of them was the elimination of the internal management training program.

I was *devastated*! I had worked so hard to make sure I was doing my part to qualify and maintain order in the department during those trying times, and just like that, with the stroke of a pen and a board meeting vote, my future was yet again uncertain. *So what happens now?* I sat in my living room staring at my desktop computer across the room and contemplating the direction of my life.

The music in my head played softly, and I heard my son come in after playing outside. I had about two hours to get him fed and situated before taking a nap and heading to my night job. Home ownership was a wonderful thing, but no one told me how much work it was to maintain one. I thought my days of working multiple jobs were behind me. The short drive to my second job was a stressful one.

I had another fight with my boyfriend and was contemplating cutting my losses and ending the relationship. It had been my second and second-longest relationship, and dismissing it was not something to be taken lightly. As if the spirits of the universe (yup, I was that person at the time) moved on my behalf to encourage the breakup, strange things happened throughout my entire work shift.

The first thing was when one of the night shift county sheriffs took an interest in me and decided to make his intentions known. His demeanor was verbally forceful and demanding, but he had an exact plan for what he wanted for his next move into politics. At the time, I had no aspirations to be anywhere near politics, and his method of approach was off-putting to me with no sign of gentlenesss, only an iron fist.

All I could envision was a life of smiling in public while potentially fighting daily sadness behind closed doors. I had no intentions of becoming the wife of a controlling and seemingly intimidating man, according to my perception of him at the time. The second strange thing that happened was that it was a *very* slow night, so I had a lot of time to think.

I decided to make a list of all the qualities I wanted in a husband and the future I wanted to have for myself. When I did the math, no man around me, including my current boyfriend, matched my expectations and financial needs. That was a real eye-opening revelation. I had to make better decisions in my life, and I needed to make them soon.

The last strange thing that happened occurred toward the end of my shift. Customer traffic had picked up in preparation for the morning commuters heading to work. I overheard two gentlemen speaking reprehensibly about the insurance company I worked for. To my surprise, I felt insulted by the comments and sensed a need to defend the company. I didn't realize I cared so much about the company's reputation. I immediately sprang into action with my quick-witted, sassy tone and set them straight with a smile.

By the time I got to my car to head home for a shower and wardrobe change, I had decided on my next steps in life. Step 1: break up with boyfriend and respectfully decline officer politics. Step 2: keep my day job and quit my night job. Step 3: graduate and receive my MBA with honors, and Step 4: stop worrying about the future.

PTSD AND ME

It is one thing to say you are going to stop worrying about the future, but it is a whole other ball game to put it into practice. Somewhere along the way, I convinced myself that I was doing the best I could to provide for my son and help other family members when possible. Little did I know that I was a ticking hormonal time bomb waiting to go off in a nuclear cloud.

As the victim of a horrific childhood trauma, my ovaries grew with an abnormally thick outer layer (polycystic), my cervix was soft, and my pelvis was tilted. It is a true miracle I even carried a child successfully to term. Top this off with repeated traumatic childhood experiences that suppressed my emotional stability.

Like a soldier waking onto a battlefield every day, I was emotionally numb with high levels of testosterone in my system for the majority of my life. What did that mean? I suffered from a permanent yet controllable hormone imbalance.

How did I know this? My endocrinologists said so, and years later, my mental health therapist confirmed the symptomatic behavior. What did they leave out? That I had suffered a phantom pregnancy induced by a psychotic break. How did that happen? Let's explore it.

You've all heard about or experienced the mood swings, uncontrollable crying, outbursts, and frustrations of a teenage girl or a pregnant woman. I will not speak for others, but for me as a pregnant teen, I didn't have the same level of emotional fluctuations because my daily focus was survival.

Fast-forward to my mid-20s, a good eight years after the birth of my son, when I arose from a good night's sleep to find my breasts tender and my belly swollen. I had been noticing a certain roundness developing in my frame over the last few months, but this rapid growth seemed to appear overnight. I waddled over to my master suite bathroom for a hot, steamy shower to get my day started.

The shower was a very painful process that took longer than expected due to the tenderness and limited range of my reach. I stepped out of the shower and began to dry off, starting with my face and working my way down to my feet. I bent forward fully to dry my feet, only to notice a few droplets of wetness reappear on the tops of my feet after I had wiped them off.

Staying in this position, I wiped my chest and my feet again, waiting to see if the wetness reappeared once more. After a few seconds, I saw the droplets leave their place of origin and fall with a gentle splash. Mortified, I stood up and caught a glimpse of myself in the medicine cabinet mirror. Unsatisfied with my limited view, I moved briskly back into my bedroom where there was a full-length mirror.

I couldn't believe my eyes. I blinked, turned side to side, and blinked again. I looked six months pregnant, and a white, cloudy liquid was dripping from my breasts as if I were ready to nurse. I made my way to the doctor's office and waited frantically to see him. I explained my symptoms, stumbling over my words. He laughed and told me it's okay and that I didn't have to be ashamed of my pregnancy.

Was he serious? Didn't he hear a word I said? I had been celibate for an extended period of time. Unless we were witnessing an unholy, antichrist, non-virgin Mary reboot situation, there ain't *no baby in there!* Under protest, I allowed blood to be drawn to conduct a formal pregnancy test, and I was sent on my way. I got a call the next week asking me to return to the doctor's office immediately.

Once I was there, the doctor apologized profusely and proceeded to order more tests. He gave me a referral to an endocrinologist. *I wasn't pregnant. I knew that, so what was wrong? He wasn't saying much. What was the deal?* After the doctor punched some computer keys, made some calls, and ordered several nurses into action, he sat down in front of me on that annoying little rolling stool and told me he suspected I had pituitary cancer.

For the next two months (back when insurance was concerned about health and not cost), I had an MRI and was poked, prodded, drained, and x-rayed into a frustrated ball of madness, only to discover that no traces of cancer were present in my body. *Okay, so no pregnancy, no cancer. What was it, then?* I shuffled off to the endocrinologist's office to undergo a series of hormonal and lymphatic tests.

My estrogen was fine, but my testosterone levels were three times higher than normal. Another slew of testing occurred to try to find the source that was causing this imbalance, but all the results came up negative. I was given a medication that over a year's time brought my hormone levels back to normal ranges. My endocrinologist was happy with the results but wanted to give me a nonmedical treatment I could do on my own.

With this method, I would only come back for annual checkups to get my hormones retested. *Sign me up. What is it?* His recommendation was to remove all stress in my life, lose weight, get into a relationship (preferably married), and have regular sex four to five times a week for the rest of my life.

STRESS MANAGEMENT

As an obedient person, I tried my best to follow what the doctor had prescribed. I lost weight and got into a relationship that I thought was truly going to lead to marriage, but it did not work out. To reduce stress, I started hanging out and made friends who had similar interests. Shortly after this lifestyle change, stress at work began to pick up in a crazy way.

My solution to work stress was to get a doctorate degree. I wanted to know how to help solve massive organizational change-related problems efficiently and with excellence. It made perfect sense at the time. I was able to use the methodologies I had learned to improve the department I was leading. These improvements, unbeknownst to my team and me, saved our jobs from elimination—a testimony of God's grace.

Somewhere along the way, my career progress caught a recruiter's attention, and I was whisked away to another state with the promise of executive training and international work opportunities. This vision was short-lived as the economic downturn hit hard like a two-ton brick. For the second time in my young adult life, I was faced with the disappointment of a corporation that did not follow through on its promises, leaving me and my son to figure out the direction of our lives.

For the sake of my son, I decided to ride things out until he graduated from high school. I figured things would eventually turn around, and even though we moved away from everyone we knew and loved, we could start fresh in a new place. To help ease the transition process, I placed my son in many after-school STEM programs and sports activities, and I pursued volunteer leadership roles in the community.

All was going well until it didn't. The company was going through so much change that the environment came to be known as the Corporate Hunger Games. Employees volunteered, if they could, to take some form of a retirement package, while others took demotions or even transfers. I was so lost and unhappy that I had to seek therapeutic counseling just to regain emotional stability.

I was miserable, lonely, and struggling to keep up with my financial obligations along with my growing teenage son. It was in these sessions that I addressed many issues of my youth and upbringing that gave me the courage to write this book and tell my story. In my quest for self-healing and workplace contentment, I resolved to allow myself to be open to a romantic relationship. I went back to my list I had created earlier and noted that all the men around me who fit my criteria and financial needs were already married.

That left me frustrated, and I was assuming pheromonal vulnerability, attracting the most unfit and inappropriate suitors who were just looking for a good time. There were two occasions I could recall where a sexual harassment lawsuit at work would have been justified. The first was when I discovered that a meeting organizer was sending out a group meeting invitation, rescheduling the meeting, and then removing some of the original invitees.

When I received the invitation and the rescheduling a few days later with a different room number, I figured it was a meeting room conflict. I didn't realize there could be an issue until I was almost to the door of the unfamiliar meeting room. The location was in a remote area, had poor lighting, and was hardly trafficked by passersby.

I didn't want to make any assumptions, but I was cautious as I entered the room. I was the only one in there since I typically arrive at meetings about 15 minutes early. After a few minutes, the meeting organizer made his appearance. He made his best attempts at flirtatious advancements, and I deflected his efforts by keeping the focus on business.

The meeting progressed as it would have if all the participants had been present, and I went back to my workstation with confidence. Attempting to forgive and forget, I accepted his later apology and agreed to ride with him to meet some coworkers for lunch. I confirmed with the other parties the lunch details and their attendance. The married suitor was not an aggressive or threatening man, and paying for lunch was a common workplace practice in order to express an apology.

I made it clear that I was not interested in anything but a professional relationship with a married man, arranged marriage or not. To my disappointment, this outing turned out to be another attempt to get me alone. Instead of taking me to the restaurant, he pulled into a motel and got out of the car.

Is he serious? What is it with men driving me to hotels? How much money do I need for a first offense bail bond? My signals of blind rage presented themselves as my anger rose. I took a moment to calm myself, allowing the soft music in my head to play before preparing for war.

I got out of the car and faced him. He was not a kidnapper, and I was *not* his victim. I calmly expressed my displeasure at the turn of events and indicated that it was in his best interest to return me to our place of employment. He looked at me, took one more drag of his lit cigarette, flicked it aside, and complied with my wishes.

Convinced more than ever that I needed a relationship to solve my pheromonal and hormonal problems, I was a woman on the hunt for Mr. Right. The movie *Just Wright* came out during that period to further illustrate or perhaps mock my pain. There were a few suitors of interest who may have been compatible with my personality, but the financial burden of my school loans would kill any hopes of maintaining a decent standard of living by men earning an average or even above average wage.

So many marriages end because of financial issues, and I didn't want to start a relationship by engulfing a good provider in a proverbial financial black hole—a six-figure school debt that could not be taken lightly. So I digressed and added two more stress factors: relationships and money. I tried to alleviate these two stressors by relocating once again to a new state with the promise of love, prosperity, and the infamous American dream, complete with apple pie.

It was clear by this point that I had a real delusional perspective when it came to optimism, but this was the same perspective that drove me to accomplish the seemingly impossible. No matter how many times I was lied to, misled, or not considered by a company or individual, I always kept pushing forward for the betterment of my son's future.

I now understand that this was God's design and order for my life. I didn't know it at the time, but my unquenchable quest to not settle in my disappointment or mistakes led to the most prolific journey, my spiritual growth.

UNINTENDED CONSEQUENCES

L et me be transparent. I had no intention or preset notion to embark on a spiritual journey. I just had a general understanding that if what I was currently doing was not working, then in order to get a different result, I had to do something different—anything different. I was sitting in my third-level apartment of my new city trying to figure out how I kept making the same mistakes in romantic relationships.

This time was supposed to be different, but it was more of the same—lies, empty promises, and no accountability while I optimistically believed every word. *What happened to "a man's word is his bond"?* Oh well, I decided that would be the last time I took a man, any man, at his word. It would only be actions from here on out. *So what do I do now?* Once again, I was sitting and contemplating the direction of life for me and my son.

It was his senior year of high school, and I could tell this move was going to cost me a lot more than my entire 401(k) plan. I heard through the grapevine that I had family living nearby. I completely forgot about my cousin and quickly made the connections necessary to reach out. Her love for the Lord and fiery advocation for her church compelled me to attend a service one Sunday afternoon.

Why not? Even though my mom was a practicing Muslim for most of my adolescent and adult years, I remembered my prepubescent Baptist roots. My fondest memories of my hometown church consisted of dressing up real pretty for Easter and gathering at my grandmother's home afterward to enjoy a houseful of goodies, all homemade from scratch with a pinch of love for flavor.

A smile came across my lips at the memory of my grandmother in her white nurse's uniform with white tights and hospital shoes, her hat pinned just so amid the sea of silver curls. "When all else fails, try Jesus!" That was a phrase I heard somewhere in my youth, but I can't recall the speaker or author.

I decided to give this church thing a try. Instantly, I felt the love of a family and the correction of a father. I was hurt, broken, angry, and afraid. I had just moved more than a thousand miles from everyone and everything I loved for the second time, only to be faced with ridicule, manipulation, deceit, and unfounded accusations.

The Holy Ghost got all up and through my flesh, and I gave my life over to Christ Jesus and accepted him as my Lord and personal Savior. I had to make a permanent change for the sake of my son and my sanity. I was baptized and became an official member of Heavens Harvest Ministries, but that was only the beginning of my journey.

I remembered my pastor, Thomas A. Pulliam Sr., saying, "You did not make a mistake moving here; God has a purpose for you in this gospel," and I took his words to heart. Since then, I have cut ties with anything and everyone not aligned with my decision to follow Jesus Christ.

Letting go of a failed relationship was easy. The hard part was taking a look at myself and conducting what Joy Ellerbe, host of the *Titus II Show*, calls a "spiritual audit." This is a daily process that compares my behavior to the instructions and principles given through the Word of God to determine if I am living with integrity. The *Titus II Show* was established by God through our pastor as a platform to spread the gospel of Jesus Christ.

"Let your heart therefore be perfect with the LORD our God, to walk in his statutes, and to keep his commandments, as at this day" (1 Kings 8:61). I slowly learned how to exemplify the love of Jesus Christ by living holy and righteous, being born again of the water and of the spirit through the teachings of Pastor Pulliam and studying the King James Version of the Bible.

By applying what I learned to my life, I was able to reconcile relationships with both my parents and honor them according to the Word of God. I now walk in forgiveness, have more patience, and follow tips to help me extinguish my anger when it rises. I am by no means claiming to be perfect, but I am striving daily to press toward the mark.

I wake up every morning with the intent to live more perfectly than the day before. James 4:17 says, "Therefore to him that knoweth to do good, and doeth it not, to him it is sin." Because of the teaching I am receiving, I can express gratitude for every trial and test given to me for more than 40 years. The impurities of my past are now cast away, leaving me vulnerable, pure, and open to receiving the future God has for me.

I bind up any evil thing that tries to come against me and release wisdom through obedience to God for success in His perfect will. The Holy Bible provides the foundational instructions for daily living with humanity, community, governance, and spirituality, each a necessity in building strong and healthy relationships.

My personal relationship with God is extremely important to me, and His Word is my primary source for all things. I have increased my faith and understanding to live a successful life that is pleasing to God no matter the cost as I live in this world. In His perfect will, I am now a professor, a dual-doctorate achiever, an entrepreneur, a public speaker, and the author of multiple works, and I am just getting started.

Without God's protection and direction, my pastor's spiritual guidance, and my obedience to do God's will, this book and the peace I have in my life would not be possible. "But none of these things move me, neither count I my life dear unto myself, so that I might finish my course with joy, and the ministry, which I have received of the Lord Jesus, to testify the gospel of the grace of God" (Acts 20:24).

APPENDIX

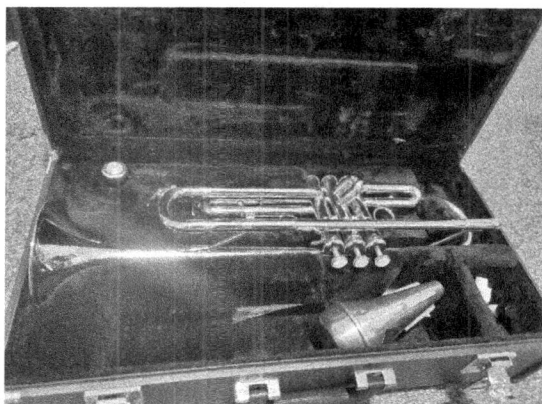

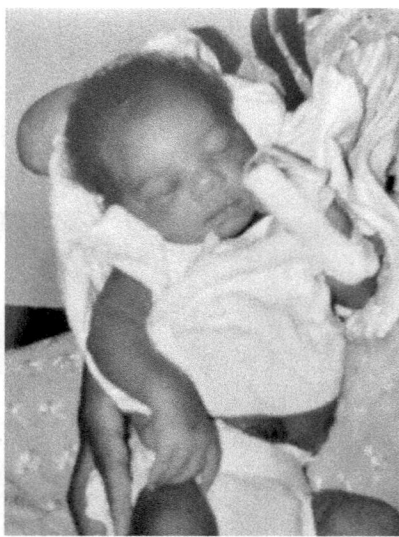

May 1996 – Dale Davis
Pacers Basketball Player
Indianapolis, IN
Scholarship Award Ceremony

Tune in to the Titus II Show!
With special guest,
Elder Thomas A. Pulliam, Sr.,
Pastor/Founder of
Heavens Harvest Ministries, Inc.
Tuesday
July 21, 2020
@6:30 PM
Facebook Live
FACEBOOK.COM/TITUSIISHOW

THE
TITUS II
SHOW
with Joy Ellerbe
New Episode this Friday!
Tune In!
Friday, December 4th
@ 7PM EST
Facebook.com/titusIIshow

WE ❤ YOU
Pastor Thomas A. Pulliam, Sr.
and call you blessed!

Jennoa Graham

Fights are started for no good reason

Tech High School seems to be the largest target of the media. Many years ago, during the '60s and early '70s, students and non-students took advantage of the school's space and freedom. Also during that time, hate was widespread over the area. Due to the combination of the environment and the population's attitude, the result was that numerous crimes were committed. The main crime at that particular time was assault.

The school board has records that statistically show a drop in violence in schools since 1960. Three decades ago, people fought because of racial issues. Whites hated blacks because they were different. Blacks hated whites for hating them and treating them like animals.

Back in that time period, everyone fought because they thought they had a right to protect themselves, which they did have the right to do, but now they see that they were fighting the wrong people for the wrong reasons.

Today people fight because they want to. A person bumps into another person, which results in harsh words. Soon a little spat turns into a all-out war. Guns and other vicious weapons are used, causing mass destruction and chaos.

The number of people who fight because they have to has decreased. The citizens who want peace greatly outnumber the ones who do not. Therefore the number of fights dramatically has decreased.

This leaves only the ones who fight because they want to. They go around looking for trouble because they have nothing better to do or it makes them feel as if they are in charge.

Crime at Tech at the present is almost nonexistent. In my three years here, there have been few fights and even fewer arrests. This year at Tech, there have been a few thefts so far, but othe. than that, nothing serious. Granted, there have been a few cases of arson in the past. Many other schools also have them. Overall, there has been very little crime at Tech and at other IPS schools.

As far as reputation goes, Tech has the worst. Unfortunately, many people feel that what happened 30 years ago still holds true in the present. Very few people have witnessed the progression of Tech through the years.

One IPS policewoman who graduated from Tech is now assigned there and can bear witness to its 22 years of progress. She is stationed at Tech through school hours and beyond on a daily basis.

Sgt. Donna Anderson says, "In the last six or seven years, there have been no serious crimes. The students on the Tech campus have had no major behavior problems." She, too, was intimidated by the size of Tech's grounds, not only as a policewoman but as a student. She remembers the hardships of the '60s and '70s — the riots, the fights and the commotion.

She makes it clear that contrary to popular belief, Tech did not have an officially segregated cafeteria. There were two cafeterias, and whichever one a person wanted to go in, that is the one he or she went into.

The media seem to take pleasure and great interest in spreading the negative all around. What about the positive? If a school has been improving, shouldn't the media advertise that, too?

Graham is a student at Tech High School.

TEENS
Continued from Page 1

the lives of their children.

This year marks the 10th anniversary of the Vivian Smith Teen Parenting Program, and the 10th year that Armstrong-Smith has been at the heart of the nonprofit program. But the 43-year-old executive director is nowhere to be found as a movie crew films a video for the program's anniversary celebration.

That's her choice, preferring to have the video focus on those she considers the program's real heroes: the former teen-age mothers whose lives have become success stories, including Tessa Reed, the 26-year-old mother of three who now sits on the sun-drenched deck of the Vivian Smith House at 4717 Central Ave., telling her story to a three-member crew from Final Cut Video.

The taping session is similar to Reed's own life — a lot of mistakes and false starts before the pieces start to come into focus. She shares how her daughters are 9, 8 and 5, that the older girls are honor students, that she has been married five years, that she runs a before-school and after-school program for Pike Township, that her life is hectic yet blessed.

And when the taping stops, Reed is asked about the influence Armstrong-Smith has had in her transformation from a 16-year-old single mother who thought her life was in ruin.

"Mary is worth a million dollars," she says. "She was more than just a mentor. She gave good advice and she had good ears to listen. She's very dear to me, you understand?"

Reed is one of the first women who Armstrong-Smith worked with, one of the young mothers she helped after leaving a well-paying job with a vacation-condominium-exchange business that would have led to free vacation lodging twice a year in such places as Hawaii, Bali, London, the Canary Islands.

"I have no regrets. This is where I want to be," Armstrong-Smith recalls as she relaxes in an office that was once a little girl's bedroom. "I had this epiphany one day when this lady was screaming at me on the phone because she couldn't get to the Caribbean for Christmas. I thought, 'Hey, lady, get a grip!' I also thought, 'I need to get out of this.' Then three different people I knew told me about this job helping teen-age parents."

She started in July 1989, and soon learned the uncertainty and heartache that often come when children have children. One of the hardest times came when the father of one of the children in the program was killed in a car wreck, just a week after his 18th birthday.

"At the funeral, his 4-year-old son took one of our staff up to the casket and said, 'That's my dad. He

was in a car wreck. If I call my dad's pager number, he'll call me back.' That's how he always got in touch with his father. It was awful. It took the little boy a long time to understand that his dad was gone."

From heartache to humor

It took Armstrong-Smith a long time to understand she couldn't save every teen-agemother who came into the program. After three years, she was in danger of leaving the work from burnout when she decided to challenge herself by doing stand-up comedy.

She draws humor from her real life, including her own struggles with the world of dieting. "I don't like being on a diet, but I don't like little women who try to sympathize with me — like the ones who shop for belts in the headband department."

Her humor also turns to God and the possible difficulties that would come if he resorted to using voice mail.

"When I was a kid, my mother always told me God hears every prayer. But when I'd pray real hard for something I wanted real bad and nothing happened, she'd say, 'Sometimes, God's answer is no.'

Well, that's real convenient. So the next time she asked me to take out the garbage, I ignored her because sometimes my answer is no.

"But what if our parents were wrong? What if God doesn't hear every prayer at the moment you pray it? What if he has voice mail and he never checks it? You're 42, your needs have changed, you look out front one morning and there's a Shetland pony."

She says humor gives her work a sense of perspective and even protection against the realities confronting the young women she tries to help: that 80 percent of teen moms nationally live in poverty, that there were 2,147 babies born to mothers between the ages of 10 and 19 in Marion County in 1996, that the Indianapolis teen birthrate is higher than the national average.

"We use a lot of humor here because you have to, to cope," she says, referring to the rubber chicken, the stress-release toys and the humorous sayings that fill her office.

"We see some things that are really sad, and this makes it easier. Before I started doing comedy, I was heading toward burnout because I thought I couldn't change people. Now I realize you can't

change people but you can create an environment where they can change themselves."

From darkness to dreams

The movie camera now focuses on 20-year-old Jennoa Graham and her 4-year-old son Andre. Four years ago, Graham first walked into the Vivian Smith House, where a small sign is now taped to the front door: "Speak delicately, dreams are inside."

Graham has lived the dreams of the program. She is one of the 67 percent of the program's participants who have graduated from high school and one of the 97 percent who have avoided a second pregnancy. She is one of the 50 percent of graduates to seek higher education. She even received a college scholarship. And she's on schedule to graduate from St. Mary-of-the-Woods College in December, with a degree in accounting and an ambition of becoming an FBI agent.

"I was a little intimidated when I first came here," Graham recalls. "Mary was wonderful. She was like a den mother to me. Everything has fallen into place, like it was meant to be."

The past 10 years have also brought change for Armstrong-Smith, including a symbolic tattoo on her 40th birthday: a tulip.

"It's on my shoulder," she says. "When I speak about the kids I work with, I sometimes liken them to seeds. One time, I handed out tulip bulbs to the audience and said, 'You plant them in the fall when everything is dying. And they have to survive the cold and darkness of winter before they can bloom in spring.' So it is with us. We have to go through periods of dark, cold and testing to become what we are."

More than anything, the past decade has taught her that the blooming process is longer for some than for others.

"My definition of success and failure has changed. When we call something a failure, it sounds so permanent. But life isn't like a test in school. You can always try again.

"We had a young mother here who dropped out of school, dropped out of this program, had more children and went on welfare. By every definition, she was a failure. But everything had changed when I talked to her a few months ago.

"She had her high school degree, she has a job that pays fairly well and she just bought a house.

"Mother Teresa said you can see God in everyone's face. I see that with our kids, with our mothers, with our families. I don't always see it perfectly, but I'm more acutely aware of it now. When you see someone turn their life around, there's an element of the sacred to that. A place where children can grow safely is sacred, too. The whole world should be that way."

STILL SMILING: In her 10th year of leading the nonprofit program for teen parents, Mary Armstrong-Smith visits with Mahogany Carson, 14, and her son Daveaun, 1.

Student overcomes adversity to win scholarship from Pacers player's fund

By Rebecca Bibbs
STAFF WRITER

When 17-year-old Jennoa Graham gave birth 18 months ago to her son, Andre, the future of her education was uncertain.

"After I had my son, it was hard going to school and juggling a newborn," the Tech High School senior said.

With the help of her family and teachers, who provided her with temporary home schooling, Jennoa rose to the challenge.

On Thursday, she became the first Indianapolis recipient of a $10,000 scholarship from the Dale Davis Foundation, established by the Indiana Pacers player. She will use the money — given in $2,500 increments for each of four years — to study accounting at St. Mary-of-the-Woods College near Terre Haute.

Jennoa's scholarship was announced Thursday during a news conference in Mayor Stephen Goldsmith's office.

Jennoa was one of three recipients of the award. The other two recipients are in Atlanta and Toccoa, Ga., Davis' hometown.

Indianapolis Public Schools Superintendent Esperanza Zendejas,

"A lot of times in our community, youths have skills that aren't recognized," Dale Davis said.

a member of the foundation's board, commended Jennoa for not giving up.

"She's a story of perseverance, she's a story of motivation and she's a story of success," Zendejas said.

Jennoa's mother, Janet Graham, said she never doubted her daughter.

"I believe my daughter has made me the proudest mother on the face of the Earth. I have always told her, 'All there's to it is to do it,' " she said.

Davis, whose previous involvement in charitable activities includes serving as a spokesman for Mothers Against Drunk Driving, said he started the foundation to help at-risk kids.

"A lot of times in our communi-

ty, youths have skills that aren't recognized," he said.

Dale Ratermann, vice president of the Pacers, said Davis also has been involved in a similar foundation run by the ballclub.

"We hope to partner up on a project or two," he said.

In addition to the scholarships, the Dale Davis Foundation is committed to a cultural enrichment program to help reduce violence and illegal drug use. It also runs a summer basketball camp, Davis said.

Fund-raising events for the scholarships and programs include a dinner and roast, a celebrity golf tournament and the 1996 Dream Team Gala during the Olympic Games in Atlanta.

The first event will be the scholarship dinner and roast of Davis at 6 p.m. April 18 at the Indiana Roof Ballroom, 140 W. Washington St.

Pacer Reggie Miller will serve as master of ceremonies.

Individual tickets are available for $100. Sponsorship packages are available for a minimum contribution of $1,500 to $10,000.

For more information, call the Dale Davis Foundation at (317) 471-KIDS (5437).

References

1. Campbell, Gordon. The Holy Bible: King James Version, Quatercentenary Edition. Oxford: Oxford University Press, 2010. https://www.amazon.com/dp/0199557608/ref=rdr_ext_tmb.

2. Pulliam, Thomas A., and Ellerbe, Joy. *The Titus II Show*. 2020. https://www.facebook.com/titusIIshow.

3. Graham, Jennoa. "Fights Are Started for No Good Reason." *The Indianapolis News*, May 15, 1995. https://www.newspapers.com/image/313311352.

4. Shaughnessy, J. "A Decade of Caring: Woman Helps Teenage Mothers Reinvent Their Lives." *The Indianapolis Star*, June 21, 1999. https://www.newspapers.com/image/106424545.

5. Bibbs, Rebecca. "Student Overcomes Adversity to Win Scholarship from Pacers Player's Fund." *The Indianapolis News*, March 23, 1996. https://www.newspapers.com/image/313274146.

ABOUT THE AUTHOR

Dr. Jennoa R. Graham was born a Hoosier in Indianapolis, Indiana, and currently resides in Atlanta, Georgia. She is not yet married and is the proud parent of her adult son. Dr. Graham is an entrepreneur and holds several degrees, including a dual doctorate. She is also a public speaker, author, and an occasional trumpet player. As an impoverished teen-parent survivor, she has developed tools to navigate out of an environment of economic hardship and emotional instability. Her perseverance in life and faith in God combine to help others press forward and achieve greater things for their families.